REVITALIZING AMERICAN LEARNING

A New Approach
That Just Might Work

For information about ordering or adopting this book, write or call:

Continuing Education Division
Wadsworth Publishing Company
10 Davis Drive
Belmont, California 94002
(415) 595-2350 in California, (800) 227-8354 outside California

THE WADSWORTH CONTINUING EDUCATION PROFESSIONAL SERIES

Power and Conflict in Continuing Education: Survival and Prosperity for All?
sponsored by Wadsworth Publishing Company and the National
University Continuing Education Association

Power and Conflict in Continuing Professional Education
edited by Milton R. Stern and sponsored by Wadsworth Publishing
Company and the National University Continuing Education
Association

Administration of Continuing Education
by George B. Strother and John P. Klus

THE WADSWORTH SERIES IN CONTINUING EDUCATION

Revitalizing American Learning: A New Approach That Just Might Work
by Herman Niebuhr, Jr.

Building Success in Math
by Carol R. Langbort and Virginia H. Thompson

Computer Chronicles
by H. D. Lechner

Air Transportation: A Management Perspective
by Alexander T. Wells

An Invitation to Fly: Basics for the Private Pilot
by Stanford Gum and Bruce Walters

Workbook for An Invitation to Fly: Basics for the Private Pilot
by George Semb

Viewer's Guide for An Invitation to Fly: Basics for the Private Pilot
by Karen Bisgeler and Jacqueline Waide

Airport Planning and Management
by Donald I. Smith, John D. Odegard, and William Shea

The Promotable Woman: Becoming a Successful Manager
by Norma Carr-Ruffino

The Job of the Planning Commissioner, Third Edition
by Albert Solnit

Project Approval: A Developer's Guide to Successful Local Government Review
by Albert Solnit

Are You a Target? A Guide to Self-Protection, Personal Safety, and Rape Prevention
by Judith Fein

PCP: The Devil's Dust—Recognition, Management, and Prevention of Phencyclidine Abuse
by Ronald L. Linder, Steven E. Lerner, and R. Stanley Burns

REVITALIZING AMERICAN LEARNING

A New Approach That Just Might Work

Herman Niebuhr, Jr.

Wadsworth Publishing Company, Inc.
Belmont, California

Continuing Education Editor: Philip Alan Cecchettini
Production: Mary Forkner, Publication Alternatives
Text Designer: John Edeen
Copy Editor: Ellen Guethlein Silge
Technical Illustrator: Dick Kharibian
Cover: Bruce Kortebein, Design Office
Consulting Editor: Milton R. Stern
Developmental Editor: Janet Felix

Printed in the United States of America

1 2 3 4 5 6 7 8 9 10—89 88 87 86 85

Library of Congress Cataloging in Publication Data

Niebuhr, Herman.
  Revitalizing American learning

  Bibliography: p.
  Includes index.
    1. Education—United States.   2. Education, Higher—
United States.   3. Industry and education—United States.
I. Title.
LA210.N53 1984   370'.973   84–11853
ISBN 0-534-04071-3

To Judi,
the best friend
I've ever had

Contents

Preface

This is a book about the state of human learning in America and what I think needs to be done to improve it. It is not a scholarly book, although it is consistent with available knowledge and research. My basic message is that we are in the throes of a fundamental shift in the learning process and that we can speed the shift through a series of personal and institutional adjustments. Although I am optimistic that our national vigor and vitality can accomplish the necessary adjustments, we just could fall short. The challenges facing us are substantial, they are poorly understood, and time is short. Therefore I have written a tract that outlines what we must do. I hope it is a prudent and useful tract.

There are many roots to what I have to say, and the reader will learn of them as he or she moves through the argument. But the precipitating insight that led me to say my piece was the discovery, some eight years ago, that American higher education was in deep trouble and that no adequate plans were being developed to save it. Because I believe that American higher education, with all its defects, is one of the great inventions of all time, I set out to understand our troubles and see whether there was a way out. In time the solution revealed itself. It was simple enough and required no vast restructuring of the domain or new resources. It just required that we think about human learning in a more fundamental way and try to extricate ourselves from some of our Rube Goldberg-like beliefs.

But the problem with the solution was that it required that all of us, all 225,000,000 of us, and all of the mainstream institutions rethink the way we manage the learning tasks of an advanced society. A quixotic adventure to be sure, but I now believe that we are going to pull it off. We are moving through a fundamental shift in the way we learn to run our lives, our families, our communities, and our economy. The most mind-boggling part of this transformation is that the American business corporation is leading the way, even though it never sought that role.

ix

I was born with an optimistic gene, though things could still go the other way. We all have a lot of work to do. But it could be fun-work once we understand what needs doing. After you finish the book, you'll say it's all very obvious and commonsensical. True enough, but sometimes the obvious needs rediscovering.

My work over the past eight years has built on the insights and advocacy of many wise and thoughtful commentators on the American condition, and I have sought to speak my debt to them in the pages that follow. More immediately, I am grateful to a small band of Temple University faculty who had the courage to transcend the conventional wisdom and develop a vision for the renewal of that institution. They include Bob Schwoebel, whose inventive spirit belies the Renaissance historian; Nettie Bartel, whose Russian Mennonite indoctrinations (like mine) dominate her cool professionalism; Ralph Towne, who embodies the best of the questing liberal arts traditions; and Judi Stoyle, whose smiling presence cloaks the no-nonsense mind and sturdy will of her New England ancestors.

I am in great debt to the hardy band of pioneers with whom I worked in the creation of CLEO. Sister Ann Marie Durst, Clarence Moll, and the rest of our Board have shown a level of leadership that has become all too rare in our domain. But I am as grateful to the folks in the trenches who helped get that unique enterprise underway: Peter Mills, Ron Watts, George Beers, Gene Kray, and, more recently, Lois Lamdin, who has tolerated the presence of a demanding change maker in altogether trying circumstances.

As the effort moved beyond the ivy-covered walls to other realms, I have been privileged to work closely with a number of people in other sectors of American life. I am especially grateful to Marc Epstein and Shel Parker, who have introduced me to the mysteries of public broadcasting, and to Hal Viehman whose persisting vision for the renewal of the church in a time of great change and whose support have given me a new friend.

At the national level I must express my deep gratitude to four men who, like my Temple faculty colleagues, show vision and courage in challenging the conventional wisdom of our field. They are Quentin Gessner of the University of Nebraska, whose leadership of the nation's continuing educators helped them to turn an important corner; Ken Young, whose quiet good sense and venturesomeness have been most helpful; Dale Parnell, who is moving the nation's community colleges into the lead in the educational domain; and Bob Craig of the American Society for Training and Development, the professional association of the nation's corporate educators, who has brought that "shadow educational system into the bright sunlight of national recognition." Thank you all. Finally, I must express my appreciation to Arlon Elser of the

W. K. Kellogg Foundation for all of his support during these interesting but trying years.

The production of the manuscript has been eased through an inadvertent consequence of participating in a computer conference organized by Jack Grayson of the American Productivity Center in preparation for the 1983 White House Conference on Productivity. If Jack hadn't introduced me to my Apple IIe and its word-processing capabilities, I never would have finished on time. And without Judi's many hours of patient editing, also on the Apple, catching all of those vague referents, we never would have made the deadline. I must also thank the blue herons of Tolchester Beach, Maryland whose slow, but determined, flights across the Chesapeake Bay during the summer of 1983 provided a useful role model for a struggling author.

Herman Niebuhr, Jr.

PART I

Although the reputation of tracts in a critical and cynical age is not one of high esteem, we would have to agree that the written or spoken tract is part of the process of moving through the great transitional epochs of history. Paul's *Letter to the Corinthians*, Tom Paine's *Common Sense*, and Karl Marx's *Communist Manifesto* were vital instruments in shaping the change process of their times. Kennedy's "Ask not . . ." part of his inaugural address and Martin Luther King's "I have a dream . . ." speech are spoken tracts that have moved millions of us in our own lifetime.

Revitalizing American Learning is written in the tradition of the tract. Although millions of us sense that American society is moving through an epoch of fundamental change, the images of where we were and where we are going are clouded for most of us. The mainstream institutions do not give us the understanding and guidance we need. But, as in other watershed periods, the adaptive and creative capacities of the species are at work. *Revitalizing American Learning* is my attempt to sharpen the understanding of the challenges we face and to describe the adaptations presently taking form. The central theme is that we are moving through a remarkable shift in the what and how of human learning—a shift that we need to understand and begin to manage.

Part I outlines the argument. Chapter One explores the need to reexamine our basic concepts of human learning. Chapter Two presents a picture of the "new American watershed" and its three very difficult challenges. Chapter Three then argues for a new, and yet very old, way to think about human learning and describes the trends leading to a strengthened learning process in the United States.

For busy and impatient readers, Part I is the heart of the argument. Part II seeks to apply the new model to all of the mainstream institutions. After Part I you could skip to the institution of your interest and let it go at that.

CHAPTER 1

A New Foundation for Learning

Let me ask the reader to think through a few questions with me.

First make a mental list of all that you've learned in your lifetime. You will probably start with the basics you learned in school or college, such as reading, writing, and computing. Then you will add other academic subjects and skills you've been taught. You'll think of history, geography, science, social studies, literature, foreign languages, and all of the later embellishments at college or university level that led to a better understanding of our past and our present. You'll think of physical education, home economics, art, music, and all of the career-related education. You'll think of all the learning you've picked up since graduation.

As you complete the list, you are likely to be impressed with all that you have learned so far. But before you put your mental pencil down, let me suggest that the list of subjects from your formal education is only the *tip of the iceberg of your life learning*!

The Life Learning Iceberg: How Much Is Intentional Learning, How Much Indoctrination?

Probe deeper. Where did the roles, values, motivations, and affective orientation that we typically sum up as "character" or "personality" come from? You will recall that your parents provided your first curriculum. They taught you to walk and talk. They taught you the early do's and don'ts of living. They taught you to trust and feel secure, and

3

some of us also learned fear, insecurity, and anxiety. Prepare to be impressed with the scope of your learning before you even got to school.

Now consider community, church, peer group, media, workplace, interest group, and other settings as well as the role you play as the agent of your own learning. Most role, value, and affective learning takes place in these settings. Because we are not aware of these aspects of our learnings and because they are such a huge proportion of them, I call them "bottom-of-the-iceberg" learnings.

For example, I have long known that my love of working with my hands comes from my grandfather's example and caring tutelage. However, I didn't understand the source of my career focus until, past fifty, I finally connected the stories my father told me about our Mennonite forebears building a society in the Ukraine to my career as a change maker.

Our Present Educational Model Assumes Life's Rules and Roles Are Taught Elsewhere

It is obvious that we learn much more than the explicit curriculum of school and college and that there are many settings in which learning takes place. Why is it that we only pick on schools when we find that our education is not up to par? Why don't we blame parents, neighborhoods, churches, peer groups, and the media as well?

To answer that question I again ask you to take up your mental pencil and note the changes in this "system of human learning" from your grandparents' generation to your own or note the changes from your generation to your children's. The fundamental design of school and college hasn't changed much within this century, but what about family, church, community, media, and the workplace? Many changes, right?

A recent immigrant family with traditions and theories of living intact probably provides a more effective setting for life learning than a fourth-generation American family with a higher level of critical consciousness. If you are an active member of a fundamentalist church or are an active Mormon, you may have an easier time "keeping it together" than most of us. If you come from an underclass background, you know the struggle to overcome the negatives of the underclass learning system.

So why don't we consider these elements of the learning process when we blame the schools? As an old psychologist, I suggest that this is a classic case of scapegoating. A better answer may be that our current concept of education has become obsolete and we don't know it.

The present educational model contains the *embedded assumption that parents, communities, churches, and the rest of the learning system are taking care of role, value, motivational, and emotional learning.* Formal educational institutions can then focus on intellectual and skill development, building on the foundation laid by the rest of the learning system. But suppose that embedded assumption is no longer valid. Suppose that the old, tradition-based foundation on which the school can build is no longer being laid.

In a Watershed Time, We Are Caught Between the Old and the New Learning Processes

I have three propositions to make in this book.

- The *first* is that American society is moving through a watershed period of fundamental change and discontinuity. The old understandings and the old ways of doing business are no longer adequate. We as individuals and our mainstream institutions such as family, church, workplace, media, and community are being challenged to adjust and reorganize.

  The most visible need is for a transformed economy which will be competitive internationally and will maintain our standard of living. Each of us needs to contribute to the transformation by becoming more inventive and adaptable and by learning new skills and abilities throughout our lives.

  The need to recreate safe and caring communities and to restore a more vital public life is a less visible but perhaps even more important adjustment. Institutions which traditionally indoctrinated us with fundamental ethical and social codes are no longer effective. We must learn our communal commitments and capabilities in a new way.

  We also need to strengthen the development of our personal and family lives. The decline of traditional indoctrinations has given us more freedom and choice in constructing our lives, but most of us don't know how to use them.

- The *second* proposition is that the national learning process within which schools and colleges provide only a small part of the necessary life learnings is in disarray and inadequate for guiding us through the watershed. The vast cultural changes of the twentieth century and especially the postwar decades, as well as the scope of the economic transformation, have undermined the learning process.

The recent rash of national reports criticizing American education underlines our failure to understand the inadequacies of the present learning process. They emphasize problems of the schools and colleges and ignore the fact that families, communities, churches, media, the workplace, and each of us as independent learners are as much a part of the learning process as the academic institutions.

- The *third* proposition is that a new, stronger learning process is being born. Many individuals and institutions have begun to meet and adjust to the watershed challenges. The megatrends of a new model of learning are in sight. If we take the time to understand what's leading us to this new model, we can organize to accelerate its arrival.

The new learning model rediscovers some ancient truths about the human species: Human learning is instrumental to goals; it occurs in many settings; and it has many modes. The adjustments required of us as individuals and of our mainstream institutions are modest and do not require vast expenditures. But they do require that we replace our present concept of education with a new understanding of human learning.

"Getting It Together" Is Harder Now Than It Has Ever Been

About eight years ago when I began the work that brought me to these propositions, I had no idea that it would lead to the "modest" goal of conceiving and then trying to organize a once-in-a-century update of the American learning process. As a university planner I was only trying to understand the challenges confronting my institution and American higher education and to construct some strategies to deal with them. But the more I probed, the more I became convinced that the challenges went deeper than a decline of college-age students and inadequate funding. The more I probed, the more I became convinced that the model of American education, which has served us fairly well for most of the century, was no longer adequate.

The maturing of my two daughters fed my unease. The older girl was brushed by the tail of the sixties counterculture; the other daughter came late enough to see its absurdities. Both bright, competent, attractive, and achieving people, they were finding much more difficulty than I had in "getting it together" or achieving a sense of coherence in their lives. I sensed that young men and women were confused about relationship roles. I sensed that the loss of the traditions that family, church, and ethnic group had built into my generation (and which we unloaded so disdainfully) left a hole in my children's development. Having sought to be a good parent, I could only conclude that I had had much less influence and control over their upbringing than I thought at the time. These generational stresses and strains are described in Landon Y. Jones's *Great Expectations: America and the Baby Boom Generation*.

We Need a New System; How Do We Begin?

In the mid-seventies, as I was turning fifty, I noticed my colleagues walking about campus carrying *Passages*, Gail Sheehy's book on stages of adult development. Grandmother and grandfather never worried about these stages, but we certainly did. A few years ago Daniel Yankelovich also documented this loss of old certainties and the quest for new ways of organizing our lives in *New Rules*. Now just walk into any book store and examine the titles of the extensive self-help section to discover our hunger for guidance in understanding and conducting our lives.

I became convinced that the nation's learning process was no longer adequate; we weren't learning what we needed to. Clearly we were moving into a difficult but exciting time, and I began to look around for other educators who were working on the same set of issues. No one else seemed interested in the deepening crisis facing higher education specifically and the learning process generally. Maybe I didn't look hard enough. Educators seemed spent, suffering a general malaise. It was a disquieting time for me.

Having spent my life in the "change business," I knew that an agenda for meeting the nation's changing needs would not write itself. Early warnings of difficult times ahead usually come from one or more persistent souls who keep at it until their efforts or other events bring the issue to national attention. All of my other changemaking was as an early follower of one or another pioneer who took the risks of getting the process underway. Now it seemed to be my turn to become the point man. I set about sharpening the new learning model, began writing and speechmaking, found some allies to pilot implementations of the model, and began to reach out to other spheres to build the foundation for a stronger learning system.

To Transform Our Economy, We Must "Work Smarter"

The one domain in which I recognized other efforts to strengthen the learning system was business. Early in the 1980s business leaders began to see the need for changes in the learning process. Our preeminence as an economic power was waning visibly as troubles facing the smokestack industries deepened. When the Japanese began beating us at our own game, we finally started thinking about the need to organize a more fundamental economic adjustment on the scale of the mass industrial transformation that took place in the late nineteenth century. The images of a high-technology, information-based economy were beginning to appear.

Over the past twenty years American corporations have become increasingly aware of how important the contribution of "human capital" is to their effectiveness. The scope of human resource development programs generally is unknown and unappreciated, but in-house training has been expanding continually. Some estimate the scale of investment to be in the thirty to sixty billion dollar range. Before its breakup, AT&T alone was spending more than one billion dollars a year on such programs. Former Secretary of Labor John Dunlop has characterized this corporate activity as the nation's "shadow educational system."

With a growing awareness of the relationship of human competence to economic performance, it is not surprising that America's corporate managers were the first to identify the need for a stronger learning process to speed the economic transformation. *Fortune* magazine provided the tagline when it called for all of us to "work smarter." Education began to come back as a national issue.

Politicians Begin To Connect Economic Problems with Education

A variety of politicians picked up the twin themes of economic transformation and the need for a stronger learning process during the gubernatorial campaign of 1982. Former Governor of California Jerry Brown had the keenest insight into the issues, but others were close behind. Governor James Hunt of North Carolina used the platform of the Education Commission of the States to issue a major report critical of the nation's schools and advocating a series of educational reforms. Within the space of a year, a sleepy Commission became a lively forum for new ideas. At its summer 1983 meeting twenty-two governors attended, a turnout impossible to imagine a year earlier.

In 1983 the nation heard a score of national reports criticizing our schools. Editorial writers and columnists provided their usual Greek chorus of commentary. Legislators began to mandate new standards; presidential candidates competed by bidding up the number of dollars we should throw at the problem. Educators were defensive but eager to have new resources as everyone debated the lengthening of the school day and year, merit pay, improved math and science instruction, and better teacher preparation. Although this spate of reports was very useful in drawing attention to the problem, none delved to the heart of it.

A Nation at Risk: The Imperative for Educational Reform

Consider the April 1983 report of the National Commission on Excellence in Education, "A Nation at Risk: The Imperative for Educational Reform," which builds its case on the urgency of the economic transformation but almost totally neglects the challenges of personal and community development. Like the others, it ignores other sources of learning. Its indicators of the slide in educational performance are arresting:

- International comparisons of student achievement completed in the 1970s revealed that on nineteen academic tests American students were never first or second, and, in comparison with other industrialized nations, were last seven times.

- Some twenty-three million American adults are functionally illiterate by the simplest tests of everyday reading, writing, and comprehension.

- About 13 percent of all seventeen year olds in the United States can be considered functionally illiterate. Functional illiteracy among minority youths may run as high as 40 percent.

- Average achievement of high school students on most standardized tests is now lower than in 1957 when Sputnik was launched.

- Over half the population of gifted students do not match their tested ability with comparable achievement in school.

- The College Board's Scholastic Aptitude Tests (SAT) demonstrate a virtually unbroken decline from 1963 to 1980. Average verbal scores fell more than fifty points and average mathematics scores dropped nearly forty points.

- College Board achievement tests also reveal consistent declines in recent years in such subjects as physics and English.

- Both the number and proportion of students demonstrating superior achievement on the SATs also have declined dramatically.

- Many seventeen year olds do not possess the "higher order" intellectual skills we should expect of them. Nearly 40 percent cannot draw inferences from written material; only one-fifth can write a persuasive essay; and only one-third can solve a mathematics problem requiring several steps.

- Science achievement scores of seventeen year olds declined steadily, measured by national assessments of science in 1969, 1973, and 1977.

- Between 1975 and 1980 remedial mathematics courses in public four-year colleges increased by 72 percent and now constitute one-quarter of all mathematics courses taught in those institutions.

- Average tested achievement of students graduating from college is also lower.

- Business and military leaders complain that they must spend millions of dollars on costly remedial education and training programs in such basic skills as reading, writing, spelling, and computation.

The report goes on to explore many sources of the problem and avenues leading to restoring excellence in American education. This and subsequent reports were important attention-grabbers that began to elbow the issue to the center of the national stage. But in its analysis of the problem and in its action agenda, it scapegoated teachers and schools as the overwhelming source of the problem and saw changes in schools as the primary source of the solution. I don't think so.

The Schools Can't Do It All

Anyone close to schools during the past twenty years knows that there is good and bad news. There have been many vital reforms such as the War on Poverty's Headstart Program, which has endured, and the "competency education" movement, which has not. But during this same period other cultural shifts such as the rise of peer-group culture reduced our schools' authority. Our teachers lost respect and prestige, and many, especially women, moved to other fields for better paying jobs. An adversarial labor-management climate developed within the schools when the real enemy was elsewhere.

During this period television began to consume more and more of children's time. Some currently estimate that the average four year old spends twenty-seven hours a week watching television and that the average eighteen year old has spent 18,000 hours before a television compared to 15,000 hours in school.

In the same period the structure and practice of family life changed dramatically. More divorce, single-parent families, working mothers, and self-centeredness among adults altered family life and the support of children.

Those of us who were parents in the fifties wanted to do better than our old-fashioned parents did. After all, we had the new psychology and the insights of the child development field with Dr. Spock as the new authority. Earlier eras had pioneer parents, but mass shifts in parenting and family patterns accelerated after World War II. Still, we stayed within the confines of the nuclear family, church, and community.

The "entitlement ethic" of the human potential movement reached its peak at this time as well. "The world owes me," "I am a victim," and "Why should I be responsible?" typify the trend in thinking that shook the Protestant ethic of hard work and responsibility and left the care of the economy to the "tooth fairy" or someone else.

During this period the church continued to diminish. The church's historic role in shaping character and teaching imperatives of the good life has been forgotten by many of us and even by church people as they adjust to their dwindling influence.

In fact, the traditional trio of family, church, and community was buffeted about during these stormy decades, but their importance as life learning and supporting institutions has been coming back into public consciousness and even political debate. Conservatives have seen far better than their liberal counterparts that the erosion of these institutions poses a danger to the nation. As part of the intellectual foundation for the Reagan administration, Peter Berger and Richard Neuhaus wrote a monograph underlining the importance of these "mediating" institutions. They argue that the mindless shift to big government and its faceless bureaucracies has begun to undermine these institutions. Though President Reagan himself has called for the strengthening of the trio, no effort has been organized to accomplish these goals.

The National Commission on Excellence in Education does not dwell on any of these other sources of the learning problem, nor does it call for the strengthening of other institutions to renew excellence. The school is to do it all, even though it never did and never will.

Clearly there is a crisis in our schools. The high-tech revolution will exacerbate it, and many adjustments are needed. But if adjustments are made out of context of other changes in American society and other institutions' vital role in the learning process, they will inevitably fall short of our goals.

Problems Lead to New Understanding and New Goals

Many years ago John Kenneth Galbraith observed that we are a very noisy society and that one needs to shout in order to be heard. The national reports on education served that purpose admirably. In that same essay Galbraith also observed that the successful shout typically seems to identify a new problem, when its actual subject is a new goal or aspiration. Galbraith's insight applies to the present verbal hand-wringing over American education; we are really talking about a need for a new set of national goals and a new way to understand and manage human learning.

The danger in these reports and media overkill is that we will grow bored with the education issue before we can reach the heart of it and make the necessary adjustments. We must shift the present focus from schools and colleges onto human learning in a broader context. I am convinced that a new learning paradigm with enormous implications for the way we manage our personal lives, organize our communities, conduct our politics, and run the economy is being born right under our noses.

We Must and Will Develop a New Learning Process

My central thesis is that the economic transformation, expanded freedoms and choices in our personal lives, and the decline of our community-building skills require a fundamental revision in the way we think about and arrange for human learning. I argue that we need to think about *all* of the learnings required to meet our goals and include *all* of the settings in which learning takes place if we are to strengthen the American *system of human learning*.

Our situation is not as bleak as it seems, however. Some changes already are well underway. Most of us already manage our lives differently and more intentionally than our parents did. The well-managed companies of Peters and Waterman's *In Search of Excellence* and a growing number of communities are beginning to understand what needs to be done.

I believe we are moving toward a stronger American learning system. Our institutions are beginning to clarify their goals in more explicit terms. While we have lost some important indoctrinations, we are replacing them in courses or programs on assertiveness, communications, etc. We are becoming more self-directed. We are becoming lifelong learners, and institutions are starting to coalesce to guide the system. If we understand those trends and implement a series of key strategies, we can accelerate the process and have the job done by the end of the decade.

The other good news is that it doesn't have to cost much money. With a new understanding of the life learning process we can organize a quantum leap in human and institutional productivity. A new age of human, communal, and economic possibilities awaits us.

CHAPTER 2

The New American Watershed

Watersheds of the Fourteenth, Eighteenth, Nineteenth and Twentieth Centuries

Most of us spend our waking hours doing what we have to do. We work, we spend time with our families, we have a little leisure (now mostly watching an average of twelve hours of television a week), we may do a little community work, we socialize with our friends. Our sense of what is happening beyond our immediate community is largely dictated by the media. We read the daily paper. We watch the evening news program with personable anchormen and women giving us words and pictures of that outside world. Given our routines, it is difficult to see big changes unless they overwhelm us or, more typically, until they have passed and some historian explains them to us.

Barbara Tuchman wrote *A Distant Mirror* because she thought the fourteenth-century changes exemplified the scope of the changes we are living through in the late twentieth century and sought to sensitize us to the tasks of adjustment. The cultural changes of that time were enormous, and we marvel in retrospect. But it is unlikely that many citizens of that era had much sense of the change they were experiencing. Now we know it was a watershed epoch.

If coping with watersheds is easier to see in retrospect, let's look at a few from American history.

THE BIRTH OF THE NATION: Given the oppressive nature of our relationship with the mother country and the political ideas that dominated our founding fathers' thinking, our separation from England was necessary. We then had to invent new ways to govern ourselves, a task that failed in the Articles of Confederation and had to be undertaken again in the formulation of the American Constitution.

Thomas Jefferson and his colleagues realized that self-government required a giant step forward in citizen competence, and the foundation for a stronger public school system was laid.

THE BIRTH OF THE MASS INDUSTRIAL ECONOMY: We spent much of the nineteenth century reshaping the American economy. Building on an array of spectacular technological inventions, our development took off with a burst of acceleration in the post-Civil War era. Again it was Jefferson who anticipated the rise in human competence necessary to fuel the new economy in his plan for the University of Virginia in 1825. Congressman Morrill and his colleagues laid the foundation for our system of public universities through legislation passed in 1862. My own alma mater, City College of New York, was established in 1847, and Temple University in Philadelphia, my home for twenty-six years, was born in 1884. Both institutions are examples of a long list of urban colleges which were established in response to the enhanced manpower requirements of the mass industrial economy.

Public schools received new assignments during this period as well. First they needed to "Americanize" the hoards of immigrants swelling the cities and then to raise their competency levels to meet rising economic requirements. As a result, secondary and vocational education expanded.

These adjustments were the most visible response to that watershed period, but the urbanization of the nation, the nuclearization of the family, the erosion of the church's influence, and the rise of mass media also fundamentally changed our society.

THE GREAT DEPRESSION: What this watershed period lost in scope it made up for in the pain it caused. It too required new ideas, inventions, and human understanding. John Maynard Keynes served as the thinker and Franklin D. Roosevelt as the inventor. The liberal agenda with its emphasis on human and worker rights and supports taught us to see ourselves and each other in important new ways, laying the foundation for the civil rights movement and the women's movement of the 1960s.

In each of these three watershed periods new challenges required new ideas and new social and technological inventions. Sometimes there are innovative, change-oriented institutions, as we are now seeing in the list of excellent corporations. It helps to have transforming political leadership, exemplified by Jefferson and Roosevelt and explored in *Leadership* by James MacGregor Burns.

We ought to do better in negotiating the new American watershed than our forebears did in coping with the watersheds of their times.

We have their experience to build on. We have a better sense of the change process and its management. While we still have no agency or profession for "watershed management" (and I doubt that we want one), we are close to the critical consciousness required for both personal and institutional adaptation. And we do have the national media to get the new messages and imperatives out fast. The Tylenol story of 1982 created a massive behavior change in twenty-four hours! Coping with our watershed changes undoubtedly will take longer than that but surely less than the forty years it took to bring about a strengthened learning process in that vital post-Civil War period.

The Challenge of Economic Transformation

I don't claim to be an economist, but as an individual, citizen, and educator I need to understand what is happening in our economy in order to make sound judgements in these roles. Like you, the reader, I am surrounded by conflicting analyses, pronouncements, and actions. The experts even earn Nobel prizes for opposing points of view.

The facts, however, seem clear enough:

- Having shifted from an agricultural to manufacturing to service economy, all within a century, we are now in another fundamental economic transformation based on information and high technology. We are still struggling to define and guide the transformation.

- Productivity has decreased relative to inflation and to other economies internationally; we have declined from our post-World War II preeminence.

- The American economy is more and more part of an interconnected, interdependent world economy. There seems to be growing agreement that other countries, mostly developing nations, with their lower-paid labor forces, can handle the mass production of goods better than we can, although Paul Hawken has recently challenged this belief in *The Next Economy*.

- Recognizing the scope of the economic transformation and its implications for all Americans, there is good evidence that we are willing to make changes in order to preserve jobs and maintain our standard of living. The willingness of Chrysler workers to take a temporary pay cut and recent Ford/UAW and AT&T/Communications Workers contracts show that it's possible to ease the economic transition for both company and worker.

- The economy is moving toward decentralized units of production. New jobs seem to be created more effectively in these smaller units.

- The economy is moving toward increased cooperation between labor and management as the way to improved productivity.

- The nagging question remains of whether the new economy will provide jobs for all who wish to work. We have built a society in which one's self-esteem depends on being able to have and hold a job. We have maintained this belief even though we have truncated the workforce by extending career preparation and institutionalizing retirement. At the same time the workforce has accommodated the entry of millions of women. But chronically high unemployment seems to expand after every recession, and dangerously high youth unemployment and the rapid diffusion of high technology into manufacturing and service underline the question. We have created a growing underclass and then we blame them for their condition. If the economy does not need all who are willing to work, we will need to make some very fundamental adjustments in the culture to provide a new basis for supporting and providing meaning for those left out.

Debate on the Implications of the Economic Facts

Given these facts, where do we go from here? No one is sure, but many ideas are floating around. For a while some Cassandras were willing to trade the smokestack sector for high technology, but they were silenced when the projections of high-tech employment leveled off at 800,000 and when Atari shipped its mass-production business off to Taiwan.

During the winter of 1982–83 Pat Choate of TRW Corporation caught everyone's attention with a projection that twelve to fourteen million workers would find their previously useful job skills obsolete in the foreseeable future. Members of Congress rushed to drop into the legislative hopper bills aimed at massive retraining programs. Marc Bendick of the Urban Institute and other labor economists countered with what they felt was a more realistic figure of two million, and the panic abated for the moment. With interest in retraining at a fever pitch, however, the question "Training for what?" began to be raised. If we are in a major economic transformation, it may be that 50 to 75 percent of the new jobs have yet to be invented. A job-specific training strategy and investment may have to follow an unprecedented job-creation effort.

Another debate centers on the creation of an industrial policy mechanism like that employed in Japan in which some form of government/business/labor collaboration picks winners and losers in the economic competition and invests accordingly. While our government is very much in the business of managing the economy through monetary policy, taxes, and its own consumption of goods and services, the free-market ideology of the Reagan administration would preclude an adaptation of this prototype. Concurrently, other critics report that the Japanese device isn't nearly as effective as we are led to think.

Megatrends, John Naisbett's best seller, probably has done more to herald the rapidly developing economic transformation than any book since Toffler's *Future Shock* and its successor, *The Third Wave*. Naisbett clearly has captured the image of the future in his first megatrend, the shift from an industrial to an information society. Paul Hawken's *The Next Economy* moves that metaphor to strategy, policy, and program. Hawken argues that the high cost of energy relative to the costs of labor and capital is moving us to an information economy in which it is productive to reduce materials and energy by increasing the amount of information in the total array of products and services through better design, improved engineering, longer durability, and greater utility. He contends that, rather than giving away the smokestack industries to developing countries, redesigning our manufacturing and service processes will restore competitiveness and productivity. Inventiveness, competence, and commitment of both management and labor are the keys to such an effort, and unless we strengthen the learning process to enhance these human characteristics, we may not reach the goal.

New Learning in the Corporation

Hawken's analysis describes an ongoing adaptation by an increasing number of American corporations. While some are still criticizing past failures, especially of the auto and steel industries, many corporations are inventing the informative economy. In preparation for the 1983 White House Conference on Productivity, I was exposed to the thinking of a new breed of corporate executives who lead the transformation by deepening the corporate commitment to the continuing development of its people, its human capital. The American business community's new dynamism challenges other institutions to do likewise.

The nation's colleges and universities, with the exception of the community colleges, have shunned the task of providing job-related training and education to America's corporations. This service is being provided by a new breed of corporate trainer and educator of the "shadow educational system."

The professional association of these corporate trainers and educators, the American Society for Training and Development (ASTD), is one of the fastest growing and vital organizations in the country. Its membership now exceeds 50,000, and more than 7,000 members attended the weeklong 1983 annual meeting in Washington, D.C. The printed programs at ASTD's annual meetings reflect inventiveness, vitality, and commitment in the search for new ways to strengthen the nation's human resources and the settings in which they work.

Peters and Waterman's *In Search of Excellence* reveals that corporate performance is a function of the corporate culture and its capacity to motivate and reward human inventiveness, productivity, and dedication to the company's goals. James O'Toole's *Making America Work* and Terrence E. Deal and Allan A. Kennedy's *Corporate Culture* also give examples of work environments that stimulate these characteristics. The example of Delta Airline employees raising $27,000,000 to give its company a Boeing 767 is incomprehensible to those of us who have lived in adversarial labor-management climates.

Corporate education has evolved within two decades from relatively narrow, job-linked training programs to a recognition of interpersonal, group, motivational, and organizational aspects of work performance and productivity. It has moved from the confines of the corporate classroom to the larger environment or culture of the workplace. Open management, information sharing, targeted reward, and other gainsharing systems are building a new level of motivation and cooperation. If we can move more explicitly to strengthen corporate culture, it makes sense to move similarly to strengthen the national culture and speed the economic transformation.

We are beginning to meet the economic challenge through innovative learning strategies for the workforce, or human resource component. For those of us who see business as "the bad guy," it seems paradoxical that excellent companies are leading the reshaping of human learning. It's time for the rest of us, especially educators, to catch up.

The Challenge of Personal Development

Basic to the visible challenge of economic transformation is the challenge of putting together coherent, balanced, and productive lives. Gardner

Murphy, one of the great twentieth-century psychologists and the best professor I ever had at City College of New York, wrote *Human Potentialities*, in which he explored human nature and its possibilities. He saw the species as characterized by three human natures. The first was obviously our biological nature, with its various possibilities and constraints; the second was the species need for structure, which leads us to create cultures with rules for dealing with physical reality and each other; the third human nature stems from our curiosity, leading us to question the very structures of thought and action we have created.

Our Second Nature

Our second human nature demands that we learn a "theory of living." Clearly, we are not born with such a theory, but we do have the capacity to develop a wide variety of theories and practices. Every human community, from the earliest tribe on, has organized and implemented a life learning process covering learnings such as you listed in the first chapter. We have always arranged to pass on the skills, roles, values, and affective characteristics necessary to achieve community goals, be they a primitive tribe's simple survival goals or the complex ones of a modern post-industrial nation.

As you remind yourself of all of the learnings you've acquired to make you a unique person, it's unlikely that you've thought about the aggregate learnings as comprising a *theory of living*. Our language currently offers no good word or set of words to describe our lives. My generation used the notion of personality as a summary term; my children's generation developed the unwieldy term "lifestyle," which connotes more than it denotes. My generation, heavily influenced by Freud and psychiatry, also was given to characterizing one another by clinical categories—"He is passive dependent"; "She is a hostile, castrating personality." My children's generation is more direct and honest in its descriptions of people.

Chris Argyris and Donald Schon offer a useful phrase in their pioneering exploration of theories of practice in the professions. They point out that all professionals have an idealized "espoused theory" which contrasts with the actual "theory-in-use." Their work represents part of the search for a word or concept to describe in comprehensive terms the dynamic, action-oriented way we implement our embedded theories of living.

Pause for a moment and ask yourself how you describe your life. Do you have a sense of your own theory of living? Were you a little surprised to make the list of life learnings and see how they all hung together to describe *you*? Most of us do not have an explicit theory of living, a clear road map of our own lives to determine where we are in relation to where we want to go.

Why is it that we can walk on the moon and engineer genes but still don't have a word or phrase to define our lives? For me it's simple: Most of the key life learnings throughout human history have been indoctrination-based, below the level of critical consciousness that we are just beginning to develop. We just didn't need a phrase until now.

Our Third Nature

Murphy's third human nature, the need to question our rules and structure, led the Greeks to a new level of consciousness about thought, government, and the relations of humans to one another. It led Zoroaster, Mohammed, Confucius, Moses, and Jesus to reject earlier religious doctrines and found new religions. It gave rise to the Renaissance, science, and other forms of critical intellect.

The third human nature is freedom seeking. Once the freedom to think began to be won, other freedoms followed in rapid succession. The fact that our nation is only two hundred years old reminds us how recently we acquired our political freedom. Within the past century the rise of the psychological sciences and related professions added a new dimension of freedom which leads directly to the challenges of personal development.

The New Psychology Opened the Gate for New Challenges

In the second half of the nineteenth century a number of thinkers began to conceive of the mind's development as a natural phenomenon, and Freud was their Saint Paul. Shorn of all its jargon, the message of the new psychology was that one's indoctrinations are naturally acquired through the early life learning process and that they can be changed through human intervention. This radical and optimistic message challenged the old Protestant ethic, "Gladly the cross I'll bear." One could jettison one's assigned fates by free associating on the analyst's couch for a few months or years and come out with a new personality and way of life.

But the new psychology was dangerous to the established authority of the traditional indoctrinating agencies: family, community, and church. Had Freud said simply, "We must view human learning and development in terms of a new freedom to design one's life, and all learning institutions need to support this enterprise," I don't think he would have been tolerated. But the new psychology cleverly chose to deal only with the indoctrinations which could be construed as leading to pain or problems and sheltered itself in the safety of the medical metaphor and domain.

So for the next fifty years the new psychology invaded the western and especially the American consciousness, leading to new institutions and professions to ameliorate the negative consequences of early indoctrinations, and raised the critical consciousness of people to look at their lives in radically new ways. Psychiatry, all forms of applied psychology, social work, counseling, education, child rearing, art, advertising, and even religion were affected. By now the ripples of the new psychology have gone far beyond original therapeutic objectives and are contributing to the present challenge of personal development in the new American watershed.

Where Do Freedom and Choice Take Us?

One day in 1948 while I was working at the New York Public Library, a young woman came in to register for a library card and gave her name, Tom Mix Peterson. Her parents believed that since children had to live with their names they should choose them, so at age three she chose the name of the best-known movie cowboy of the 1930s. The granting of freedom and choice to the young has proceeded apace, finding its logical limit in the British free school Summerhill, whose write-ups made for exciting reading twenty years ago.

Margaret Mead suggested in *Culture and Commitment* that the curves of the rising freedom/choice-based culture and the declining authority-based culture crossed about the time of World War II. Mead saw a millenial shift occurring: For the first time the young were no longer learning from the older generations but were designing their own culture, and the old were now learning from them. Landon Y. Jones's *Great Expectations* provided graphic details of this phenomenon as the baby-boomers invented the counterculture of the sixties.

This millenial shift has created new problems and opportunities for each of us, for families, churches, educational institutions, and all concerned with human learning. We do not yet fully understand these problems and opportunities, and in spite of many positive developments our failure to understand them has resulted in a certain amount of disarray and drift in American society.

My generation was warned early of the potentially corrosive effects of freedom and choice by Erich Fromm's *Escape from Freedom*, published in 1943. Fromm warned that freedom must be engaged with responsibility and should lead to new personal or social structures, lest it otherwise lead to anxiety and the loss of necessary structure. We had lost many of the old indoctrinations, we had gained new freedom, and unless we became more responsible for the design of our lives we would remain underdeveloped.

Walter Lippmann began to worry about this problem as early as 1915 and in 1966 made the following observation:

> They [the American people] have found, I submit, that as they are emancipated from established authority they are not successfully equipped to deal with the problems of American society and their private lives. They are left with the feeling that there is a vacuum within them, a vacuum where there were the signs and guideposts of ancestral order, where there used to be ecclesiastical and civil authority, where there was certainty, custom, usage and social status, and a fixed way of life. One of the great phenomena of the human condition in the modern age is the dissolution of the ancestral order, the erosion of established authority; and having lost the light and the leading, the guidance and the support, the discipline that the ancestral order provided, modern men are haunted by a feeling of being lost and adrift, without purpose and meaning in the conduct of their lives.

Lippmann saw the American university as the most appropriate institution to provide guidance, filling the void left by the church's declining traditional authority. He was not hopeful, perhaps having observed that the previously vital land grant institutions had withdrawn from such a guidance function. Presently fragmented and demoralized, the American university shows neither the will nor the capacity to take on this assignment. The community college may be our best hope at the moment.

We are now confronted with a larger intentional learning agenda, having seen that tradition-based indoctrinations have given way to new freedoms and choices, but most of us have not yet begun to understand Lippmann's analysis or its implications. As Gardner Murphy foresaw, we are on the threshold of new human possibilities, provided we engage the challenge of personal development.

The Challenge of Re-Creating Community

A third newly emerging challenge, that of re-creating community, is linked inextricably to those of economic transformation and personal development.

As old indoctrinations defining our communal roles and skills as well as old reinforcements for communal behavior declined, it was inevitable that the quality of communal life would diminish. Communities in themselves are an abstraction; there are only people behaving in support of communal goals.

Just as there are good companies and families, there are good communities which approach the task of community building in more intentional and explicit ways. But just as the schools cannot make it without parents and families playing their appropriate instructional and supportive roles, the same can be said for the importance of communal instruction in support of the life learning process.

As Murphy said, it is our nature to create communal structures. We need nurturance, coherence, rules, and a way to share communal tasks, though we've come a long way from the fulfillment of these needs in early tribes. Now we are ambivalent about our geographical communities; we have invented no enduring conceptual communities, and our sense of political obligation has declined. The poverty and violence of the underclass community seem to be growing. Unless we develop a new set of explicit communal imperatives, we may be left in Lippmann's vacuum.

Nostalgia and Ambivalence

At a geographical level we live in neighborhoods or communities in which informally organized associations and rules are more embedded than explicit. Some of us may be nostalgic for the "old neighborhood" or the small town we left for the Big City. Having grown up in East Harlem in New York City, then mostly an Italian Catholic, working class community, I'm not very nostalgic, but I have vivid memories of the culture of the neighborhood and the impact it had on my own development. As I have sought to understand the learning process I have become sensitive to all that I was taught by the old neighborhood at "Hun-nineteenth Street and Pleasant Avenue." You might pause for a moment and ask yourself the same question: What did you learn in the community of your childhood years?

Yankelovich's *New Rules* suggests that our nostalgia for neighborhood and community is our way of correcting for the excessive individualism of recent decades. Previous generations would be surprised by it; American novels of the twenties and thirties by Theodore Dreiser, Thomas Wolfe, Sherwood Anderson, and Sinclair Lewis portray small-town life as stifling, hypocritical, and mean spirited.

But if we have grown somewhat ambivalent about the small town and neighborhood, we certainly have developed a profound ambivalence for the big city, its anonymity and danger. Some still feel liberated and excited by it; others find triple locking doors, walking streets defensively, and being lonely outweigh the value of galleries, shops, theaters, restaurants, and museums. Most of us run in and out of New York as fast as we can.

Our ambivalence toward small towns or big cities reflects what we feel in the structure of our own lives. Urie Bronfonbrenner put it succinctly in *Two Worlds of Childhood*, in which he contrasted contemporary child-rearing practices here and in Russia, where the pursuit of individualism was nearly as rampant as it was here. Both individualism and communalism have costs and benefits, he concluded. We value individualism for its freedom, creativity, and sense of achievement, but we fear loneliness, isolation, and anomie. We enjoy a close community's warmth and nurture but abhor its tendencies to be stifling, overly controlling, and hypocritical. The balance eludes us, but we are working on it.

Nostalgia for small-town life was particularly high for many of us returning from World War II, and we took off for the new suburbs as fast as we could. We had Little League, PTA, and the Civic Association, but the tides of individualism were running high, our careers were in the city, two cars gave us mobility, and television replaced a lot of casual social contact. Soon most of us discovered that there was less community in the new suburbs than in our old neighborhoods. Even in the cities people moved off their stoops to spend their evenings in front of the television set.

In the sixties as we focused on big city problems Jane Jacobs's *The Death and Life of Great American Cities* gave some useful observations and suggestions on how to restore the good life in urban settings. She said a rich street life could be a way to rebuild communal bonds and a network of support to restore order. While year-round rich street life is probably gone forever, every big city has close-knit neighborhoods which are proud of their shared goals and values; Philadelphia's Society Hill and Queen Village have their counterparts in Washington, Boston, Atlanta, and San Francisco. Populated largely by young professionals "gentrifying" the neighborhood, these new communities, like some corporations, have cultures of excellence. The parallel is obvious, even if we are still short of the explicit strategies of community building now available to corporate management. If we can design a culture for the Frito-Lay Company, we ought to be able to do it for a community or neighborhood.

The Communes of the Sixties Were Conceptual Communities

Some of those who matured in the sixties rejected the suburban lifestyle and invented a new way of living, the commune. Soon they discovered how difficult it is to manufacture a community. But those who wish less complexity and pressure in their lives are still drifting toward rural and small-town America. At the moment we have no magic solution to the task of designing a communal arrangement to reflect a new realism, but the task remains. What do we do?

If you go back to your learning list and search for your early community indoctrinations, those of us over fifty will have a different list than most of you under thirty-five. The pre-World War II, pre-television, preyouth culture was more potent in providing instruction on the roles, competencies, attitudes, manners, and obligations of communal living than the postwar communities. Indoctrination learning in our personal development and communal roles has dropped out of the national learning system for most of us, leaving us with freedom and choice in our definition of community. Those who built communes sensed this loss, but the rest of us have yet to understand the magnitude of what has been lost.

The Underclass Community—The Least Support for Those Who Need It Most

Nowhere is the loss of vital indoctrinations more visible than in the nation's underclass communities. Ken Auletta's recent book *The Under-class* paints a vivid picture of the absence of necessary life learning among the poor. The acquisition of those cognitive, motivational, and value learnings basic to scholastic success, neighborhoodliness, and safety is declining in many of these settings. In some neighborhoods the older generation, such as the black grandmothers who came up from the South and maintained standards and structures, are gone, opening the door to the dominance of neighborhood peer groups, gangs, and hustlers. The larger causes of racism, chronic unemployment, and the indignity of welfare go unaddressed, and the tragedy of lost learnings goes on. Schools alone cannot make a difference.

Twenty years ago Michael Harrington's *The Other America* presented a similar portrait and, eliciting a sympathetic response, laid part of the foundation for the Great Society programs. Today we seem unresponsive and mean spirited toward the underclass, which is neither to our credit nor in our self-interest. If we are not to saddle the nation with a permanent underclass less and less able to participate in the information economy, we must strengthen underclass culture with the same vigor we apply to corporate culture.

The Role of Government in Community Building

Within this century many of the tasks and obligations of communal living have been transferred to government. Workman's compensation, social security, unemployment compensation, medicare, medicaid, vocational rehabilitation, public housing, and hundreds of support and service programs were all born in a spirit of communal altruism. Something has been lost in their implementation, however, and in this reactionary time we are skeptical of bureaucrats and professionals. We may even have lost some of our sense of charity and altruism. We have been preoccupied with ourselves, and there is less to go around in a contracting economy.

As hunger returns to our country, and as our president urges us to rebuild the private sector and voluntarism, we must renew our sense of the good society and its communal obligations. Family, church, and local communities used to develop this sense, and we must find a new source, whether it be from presidents, governors, or ourselves.

I have been chairing the long-range planning effort of Philadelphia's Community Leadership Seminars, which will celebrate its twenty-fifth anniversary in 1984. Since the beginning, CLS has been orienting the emerging leaders of our top businesses and other organizations to the tasks of civic betterment and leadership. We have recognized that old sources of leadership and sense of civic obligation, once taught by old families and the upper classes, have dried up, and although we have no clear answers at the moment, we know we must invent new ways to develop leadership.

Another civic problem is our waning sense of obligation to participate as politically active citizens. In 1837 de Tocqueville described in *Democracy in America* our enthusiasm for our new democracy. A few years ago, however, Richard Reeves retraced de Tocqueville's steps and found troubling cynicism and much less enthusiasm. Decline in voting participation set in long before Watergate. The fact that only 28 percent of all Americans eligible to vote made Reagan president in 1980 and the fact that the lowest rate of voting participation comes from our youngest citizens raise a danger signal for American democracy.

Probe for the source of your own voting behavior and political participation. I learned mine from my parents and neighborhood. My parents received their citizenship while I was a young boy and passed on to me a sense of strong obligation to our new country. East Harlem was run by the old Tammany Hall Democratic machine and had neighborhood political clubs in storefronts scattered through the area. As the local politicos played cards in the neighborhood clubhouse, they sent us kids out for buckets of beer and allowed us to hang around. During the World Series they'd simulate the games on the store windows for us. I learned more about politics there than in any civics or political science class.

The sense of decline in the quality of our communal, civic, and public lives has been building. There have been calls for the strengthening of civic literacy but little action, as though we don't know how to approach the question. In 1983 two fine books began to move the re-creation of community to a higher level of national consciousness, however. The first was Amatai Etzioni's *An Immodest Agenda*, in which he confirms the decline of the skills and commitments requisite to a sound society and advocates the rebuilding of our sense of mutuality and civility, especially by strengthening family and school.

George Will's *Statecraft as Soulcraft* comes to similar conclusions, but with a different argument. Will says that the founding fathers made the terrible mistake of assuming that the adjudication of contending interests was the prime task of government and built the nation accordingly. Will disputes this premise of adjudication responsibility and argues that the good society must build a sense of moral obligation in its citizens. He goes on to construct a conservative rationale for the welfare state.

Both Etzioni's and Will's books bring E. L. Schumaker's *Small Is Beautiful* to mind. Schumaker observes that some ideas are not dangerous in their own time but become dangerous later. He uses the example of value relativity as harmless among the certainties of the nineteenth century. But in a much less certain twentieth century, the "anything goes, everything is OK" application of value relativity brings us close to anarchy.

The culture of the founding fathers, passed on through traditional indoctrination mechanisms, taught them Etzioni's mutuality and civility and Will's sense of morality and coherence. A political premise which sought to deal with contending interests therefore was not nearly as dangerous or empty as it is today without these fundamental indoctrinations to give us a sense of community. The present disarray during this watershed period is not inevitable, however, if we recognize that we have the same freedom and choice for re-creating community that we have for strengthening our personal lives and transforming the economy.

Paradigm Shift

It should be apparent that no one profession or institution is ready to take charge of coping with these challenges—but then, that is clearly a basic characteristic of watersheds. Conventional thinking and practice become obsolete, as do the institutions that generate them. New ideas, learnings, and changes come from the edges and margins, not from the establishment.

Thomas Kuhn's *The Structure of Scientific Revolution* contributed the notion of the paradigm shift to our vocabulary. A paradigm shift occurs as we give up one well-established way of looking at the world for another, such as the shift from Newtonian physics to Einstein's relativity physics. Peter Drucker calls such a shifting time an "age of discontinuity"—after electricity was invented, for example, it was pointless to improve the gaslight.

Paradigm shifts, discontinuities, or watersheds generate much heat before there is light. Whether one is trying to give up smoking, transform an economy, or re-create a community, change is hard. Conflict arises as diehards refuse to see the new truth and evangelists of the new truth grow impatient with the diehards.

I hope I have not left the reader pessimistic at this point. Despite the disarray and obsolescence of most of our institutions, we are beginning to meet the challenges. With the excellent corporations in the lead, new ideas and inventions are beginning to appear in other domains. Some of the professions and institutions which were smug in the sixties, forcing us to try to solve urban problems through alternative structures, now are defensive. But that is a first step to adjustment and adaptation.

Thousands of us are working in small ways to bring a strengthened learning process to life, and megatrends toward this are already in sight. As we move on to examine these trends and the concepts within them I am reminded of Jean Revel's *Without Marx or Jesus*, a de Tocqueville-like tribute to the revolutionary nature of American society. It was published in the seventies at a time when the nation was in no mood for such a compliment, and we shrugged it off. I thought Revel was right then, and, optimist that I am, I think we'll set a record moving through the watershed. But the "tooth fairy" won't do it for us. All of us as individuals, as citizens, and as representatives of institutions have roles to play.

CHAPTER 3

The New Human Learning System

Every Society Has Organized a Life Learning Process

Periods of big change make us nostalgic for the good old days when things were settled and stable. They weren't, of course, but our yearning for certainty makes them so. In many parts of the country "back to basics" is the byword. Having taken on too many secondary functions once taught by family, community, and church, the schools are now being asked to return to teaching reading, writing, arithmetic, and maybe computer literacy.

As we have seen, the growing loss of necessary indoctrinations from the traditional institutions created a vacuum. So the schools began to take on counseling, sex education, and values clarification. But even if the expansion of school functions is understandable, it is naive to suppose that the schools in their few hours of intervention in the lives of children and young people can handle both the top- and bottom-of-the-iceberg learnings. Back-to-basics advocates have a point, but they tend to stop there and never deal with the rest of the life learning problem.

A strategy for more fundamental changes is necessary, and the following reminders might give us useful direction:

- Remember that every society since the earliest tribes has organized a life learning process. *A society's goals, be they economic, communal, or personal, determine the life learning its members must accomplish.* Learning is instrumental to goals, so when goals change, so must the relevant learning. Excellent companies and human resource development (HRD) people have rediscovered this truth, one that still eludes many institutions and individuals.

- Remember that learning occurs in many settings. The national reports keep missing this point in their exclusive focus on schools.

- Remember that there are different modes of learning. We tend to focus on the active, intentional learning of schools and colleges and to forget about the Pavlovian and Skinnerian learning that develops our roles, values, motivations, and affective characteristics.

The basic question is: *What do Americans need to learn in order to reach our goals?* When we begin to answer that question, we then ask: *How shall we arrange to have it learned?*

Every society has asked and answered these questions, but the process has been more embedded than explicit. The early tribes did not set up a committee or task force to study the questions and report recommended courses of action. Until the Greeks developed a new level of critical consciousness and the big questions could be examined and debated on a conceptual level, these questions were asked and answered through experience and traditional indoctrinations and then were passed from generation to generation. Mindless as the process may now seem, it built the foundation for subsequent cultural evolutions.

Our predecessors eventually began to deal with parts of the two basic questions more explicitly, but we are the first generation to examine them critically in their entirety. At first it may seem a horrendous task with dark intimations of Orwell's 1984 mind police, but we are already both asking and answering the questions with a new explicitness. The adjustments required of us and our institutions are modest and inexpensive and, if we can clarify our direction, can be liberating and life enhancing rather than limiting as in Orwell's vision.

The Human Learning System Is As Old As Humanity and As New As Systems Analysis

As an old (and ex) Freudian I suggest that part of our present difficulty is that we are fixated at the institutional level of development in terms of human learning. We must instead see schools and colleges as only part of a learning system. We have always had a human learning system, and though it may not have been as explicitly designed and managed as our contemporary economic system, in retrospect we can see that it worked as a system. Who can argue that the church provided embedded systems management throughout the last millenium?

We can recognize Plato's *Republic* as the seminal systems science book and can see the systems metaphor in the writings of scores of philosophers since. But the application of explicit systems thinking to planning and problem solving came to fruition during World War II and has been moving into our consciousness ever since. Norbert Wiener's *Cybernetics* and C. West Churchman's *The Systems Approach* both describe this development.

In recent decades we have learned to think systemically in many aspects of our lives. We know the economy is a system and can link local Mom-and-Pop stores to the multinationals, to fiscal and monetary policies, and all these to OPEC's oil-pricing structure. We recognize the federal system of governance in which national, state, and local governments are interconnected. We are still struggling to create a more effective international system of cooperation and conflict resolution, and we have learned to understand and respect ecosystems.

Why is it that we have yet to think of human learning as a system? It's very simple: Until recently, we didn't need such awareness. Over time the learning system evolved. The invention of schools and colleges, their subsequent modifications, and the new psychology and its applications helped adapt the system, all without a systems awareness. But now we need that awareness.

For the remainder of this book I will shift from "learning process," which connotes something larger than schooling, to "human learning system," or "HLS," as the conceptual framework for charting strategies for strengthening human learning.

Systems Awareness Is Useful in Understanding Human Learning Throughout History

In the adjacent charts depicting human learning system models of the past and present, the + and − signs indicate my view of an item's greater or lesser significance.

Chart A lays out the basic HLS model, where all societies are seen to have economic, communal-political, and personal-familial goals. These goals then mandate instrumental learning that individuals must acquire and which HLS institutions must provide in either intentional or in-

doctrinating curricula. The model describes the goal-setting part of the process and shows the source of the necessary learning.

Chart B applies the model to circa 1800 when economic realities and goals were mainly agricultural. Communal life was rural and small-town oriented. Personal and family life was tradition-based, with few of today's choices. The human learning system of that preindustrial era was dominated by the traditional trio of family, community, and church, which provided skills, role definitions, value structures, and affective characteristics to meet society's goals. Intentional learning was rising slowly in response to Thomas Jefferson's call for greater citizen competence, but formal learning for most was a short-lived, terminal activity with a narrowly defined curriculum. Much like earlier learning systems, it relied on indoctrinations and was sufficient.

Chart C illustrates the shift of the late nineteenth century to the Industrial Paradigm and defines our present HLS model. Economic reality and goals shifted fundamentally as we left agriculture and cottage industry for mass industrialization. More competent workers were needed, and we invented institutions to train them. We became an urban nation heavily populated by newcomers, and new modes of communal living and governance were required. The shift to nuclear family living and the rise of individualism and interest groups marked a basic change from tradition-based extended family life.

Then as now we criticized and reformed our formal educational institutions, but the indoctrinating institutions, still vital sources of learning, were less influential in the economic realm. Fathers still got their sons into the mills and factories, but the sons had more opportunities for other jobs and careers than their fathers. For the first time fathers could aspire to having their sons do better than they did.

Although most of the old indoctrinating mechanisms remained intact, the substantially expanded intentional learning agenda accelerated the decline of these mechanisms. The church, the embedded system manager of the traditional trio, began to lose authority and influence as it left the town center for residential neighborhoods. The industrial HLS worked fairly well for most of the century, but its mixture of indoctrinations and intentional learning led to some tension and conflict and sowed the seeds of our present disarray. The media became a rambunctious new part of the system at this time as well.

Chart D brings us up to date. The title, Information Age Paradigm, highlights the fast developing information-based economy. It summarizes much of the material covered in Chapter Two. The symptoms of the new watershed first appeared in the sixties in the civil rights, women's, and students' movements. All these showed that old power and authority relationships once maintained through indoctrination had given way to freedom and choice. We may applaud the

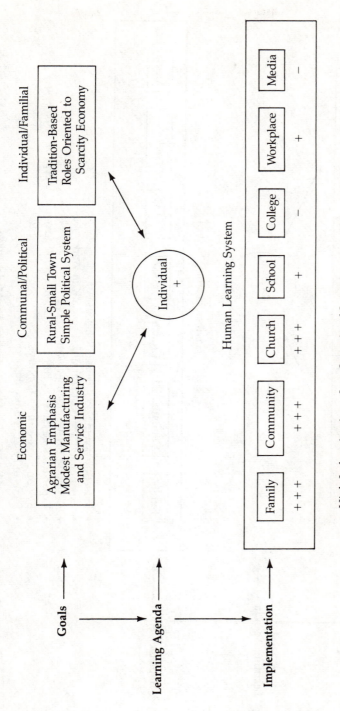

Goals →

Learning Agenda →

Implementation →

Economic

Agrarian Emphasis
Modest Manufacturing
and Service Industry

Communal/Political

Rural-Small Town
Simple Political System

Individual/Familial

Tradition-Based
Roles Oriented to
Scarcity Economy

Individual
+

Human Learning System

Family	Community	Church	School	College	Workplace	Media
+++	+++	+++	+	–	+	–

- High Indoctrination—Low Intentional Learning
- Traditional Institutional Domination
- Embedded System Management
- Formal Learning as Terminal Activity
- Curriculum Narrowly Defined
- System Inadequate to Changing Goals in Mid-Nineteenth Century

Chart B The Pre-Industrial Model (1800)

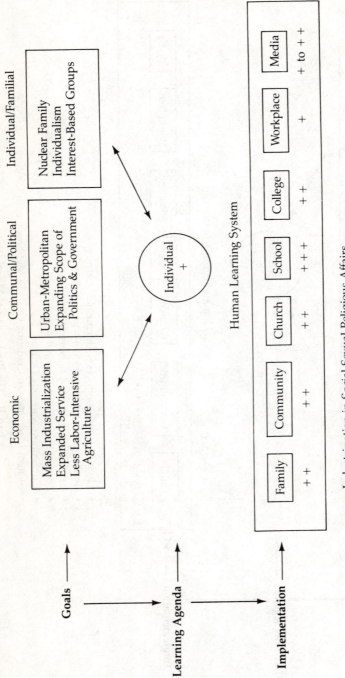

Chart C   The Mass Industrial Age Model (1900)

Goals

Economic

Mass Industrialization
Expanded Service
Less Labor-Intensive
Agriculture

Communal/Political

Urban-Metropolitan
Expanding Scope of
Politics & Government

Individual/Familial

Nuclear Family
Individualism
Interest-Based Groups

Individual
+

Learning Agenda

Implementation

Human Learning System

| Family | Community | Church | School | College | Workplace | Media |
| ++ | ++ | ++ | +++ | ++ | + | + to ++ |

• Indoctrination in Social-Sexual-Religious Affairs
• Expanding Intentional Learning, Especially in Work Areas
• Declining "System Management"
• Expanded Role-Power of Formal Education but Still Terminal, Except for Extension
• System Successful for Century!
• Signs of Disarray Since the 60s

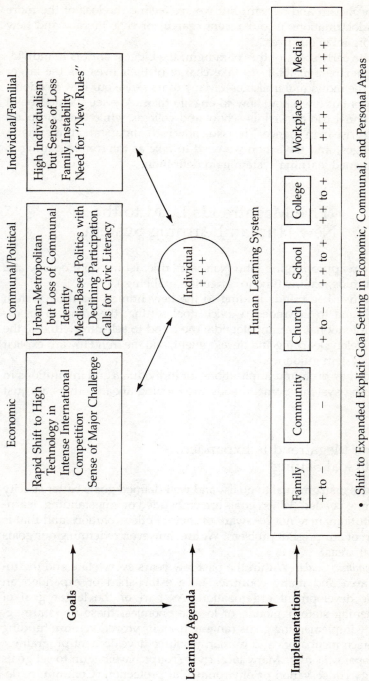

Goals

Economic

Rapid Shift to High
Technology in
Intense International
Competition
Sense of Major Challenge

Communal/Political

Urban-Metropolitan
but Loss of Communal
Identity
Media-Based Politics with
Declining Participation
Calls for Civic Literacy

Individual/Familial

High Individualism
but Sense of Loss
Family Instability
Need for "New Rules"

Individual
+++

Learning Agenda

Implementation

Human Learning System

Family	Community	Church	School	College	Workplace	Media
+ to –	–	+ to –	++ to +	++ to +	+++	+++

- Shift to Expanded Explicit Goal Setting in Economic, Communal, and Personal Areas
- Shift to Expanded Intentional Learning in Role, Value, and Affective Areas
- Shift to Self-Directedness in Learning from Authority-Centered Pedagogy
- Shift to Lifelong Learning Commitment
- Shift to Explicit Learning System Guidance

Chart D The Early Information Age Model (1984)

demise of racism and sexism, but we are feeling the loss of the more useful indoctrinations in our recent search for civic literacy and new ways to organize our lives.

In the early stage of this paradigm, the biggest shift is in individuals' greater responsibility to take charge of their lives (as the larger circle for the individual indicates). Many of us sense our new freedoms and choices but few know how to engage them. We see the decline of the traditional trio as well as school and college, while the workplace and media rise in influence. The issue now is to understand this system, its challenges, and the action we need to take as the trends leading to a strengthened learning system gain definition.

Five Megatrends Lead to the New Human Learning System

(Since I am appropriating John Naisbett's title, let me do it openly and with gratitude, as it is time for attention grabbing.)

The five key trends leading to the new human learning system are: the trend to expanded, explicit goal setting; the trend to an expanded intentional learning agenda; the trend to self-directedness; the trend to lifelong learning and development; and the trend toward explicit learning system guidance.

Each has profound implications for individuals and institutions in the learning system. Some already are moving ahead; others are just starting.

The First Megatrend Is Expanded, Explicit Goal Setting

Learning is instrumental to goals, and well-defined goals better specify the learning needed. When goals are embedded or longstanding, learning institutions may not be aware of their subtle evolution, and that is a big part of our present problem. We are, however, redefining our goals in several areas.

Economic Goals: Within the past few years every state and metropolitan area and many countries have established or expanded an economic development organization. As part of the larger goal of strengthening state, regional, or local economies, these units are aggressively implementing goals ranging from improved venture funding to high-tech incubators and human resource development programs.

Communal Goals: Many local civic groups have begun to set goals for energy conservation or environmental protection. Community development and community education programs, led primarily by school superintendents, continuing educators, and some social workers, are being planned and implemented. Community goal setting is still in its infancy, however, and short of what Etzioni and Will have called for.

Personal Goals: Many of us are expanding personal goals in one way or another. Book store self-help sections, radio talk shows, personal advice columns, and the wide range of career and life planning programs all support this trend. Much of it is fragmented, however, and only the life planning approaches are beginning to see the task in holistic terms.

The Second Megatrend Is Expanded Intentional Learning

Much of what we used to learn through indoctrination we are now beginning to learn intentionally. If one's definition of masculinity, femininity, leadership, courage, compassion, caring, inventiveness, entrepreneurship, risk taking, neighborliness, citizenship, justice, and all the other bottom-of-the-iceberg learning is to be approached intentionally, consider the possibilities! We've just begun this shift, but most continuing education catalogs or corporate HRD programs list courses in assertiveness, parenting, intimacy, interpersonal competence, group effectiveness, and the like. This trend requires more research and development to mine its potential, but it has begun to happen.

The Third Megatrend Is Self-Directedness

The trend to self-directedness is the outcome of a profound cultural drama that has been developing for centuries. Richard Sennett's *Authority* describes it in terms of shifting power and authority relationships. The drama is now evident in all aspects of our lives. We see it now as the boss becomes the open-door manager, as Father becomes Dad, as marriages shift from dominant-submissive role definitions to "significant other" relationships, and as we take responsibility for our health and ask the doctor to be our consultant.

Erich Fromm commented on this momentous shift in *Man for Himself* almost forty years ago, noting that if we resent others controlling our lives, we must be prepared to take responsibility for doing it ourselves. Daniel Yankelovich's *New Rules* and Christopher Lasch's *The Culture of Narcissism* both show how freedom from old authorities led for a time to the mindless hedonism and "entitlement" ethic of the sixties and seventies. But a more responsible self-directedness is becoming evident.

This trend has vast implications for the learning system, as compliant students who once bowed to pedagogical authority metamorphose into self-directed learners. The expanding use of computers will further this trend. It is projected that by the end of the decade ten million of us will be "tele-commuters" working at home and that millions more will be doing much of their learning via educational computer software.

Aunt Minnie's question of us when we were small—"What do you want to be when you grow up?"—is newly significant in this context. It used to be an imperative reminding us that we had to choose and work toward a career, but now it asks us to consider what kind of men and women we will become and what political stance, religion, leadership style, or other characteristics we will choose. Once indoctrinations made these decisions for us; now we must structure a life learning agenda to address them intentionally.

The Fourth Megatrend Is Lifelong Learning and Development

This trend probably is further along than any other. Between thirty and thirty-five million American adults enroll in an organized educational experience annually, and the rest of us similarly read, listen, view, and behave as lifelong and self-directed learners. In the mid-seventies UNESCO issued several excellent reports calling on educational establishments all over the world to more effectively support lifelong learning as a goal and process, and the Club of Rome's related study, *No Limits to Learning*, advocates the same objectives. Stages-of-life-development literature mentioned in Chapter One also help explore the continuing dynamism of our lives and help define where we are and where we are headed.

Most institutions still view education as a terminal activity, but community colleges have led in the removal of age barriers. The average age of their students is approaching twenty-nine, with the upper part of the range in the seventies and even eighties. The time is coming when the smart college or university will forge a lifelong learning relationship with its graduates, expanding the present limited association with alumni.

The Fifth Megatrend Is Explicit Learning System Guidance

The learning system is an old idea characteristic of all societies. Lawrence A. Cremin, retiring president of Teachers College, Columbia University, has been writing about the many settings of human learning for thirty years. Urie Bronfonbrenner, one of our top child development experts, reminded us of this in *Ecology of Human Development*, published in 1970. But what once bound institutions together in the old learning system has dissolved, and it is necessary to rediscover the systemic character of human learning and put the system together once again.

In the 1960s the Ford Foundation, under Paul Ylvisaker's leadership, dangled the foundation carrot before the nation's cities to encourage urban citizens to think, plan, and act "comprehensively." Ylvisaker's "Great Cities School Improvement Program" and the subsequent "Gray Area Program" were the first efforts to relink the fragmenting institutions into a common effort of strengthening human learning and improving urban life. That and the systems-oriented Great Society programs which followed fell short of their goals but led us in the right direction.

At that time I became responsible for brokering a relationship between the renewing Philadelphia schools and the newly developing community mental health movement, one of the Great Society's innovations. We had good will, lots of money, and no power or competition problems, but we went nowhere. We just could not bridge the barrier imposed by separate professional languages in spite of our common goal. As institutions come to see their common membership in the human learning system, perhaps we can do better.

The present frontier of learning system consciousness and bridge building stems directly from economic pressures. The need for new knowledge and skills to fuel the economy is leading to education-business partnerships around the country, from "adopt-a-school" programs to better communication between employers and educators. The 1983 White House Conference on Productivity emphasized strengthening these ties, and this trend will continue to grow.

Six Implementing Strategies

These five megatrends provide a foundation for a strengthened learning system as we move past the now obsolete Industrial Paradigm. It is now up to us to hasten the arrival of the new Information Age Paradigm with the following strategies for action:

1. Orient the Citizen Learner

Our highest priority is orienting a nation of citizen learners to the new realities and learning tasks confronting us. We know now that we don't fully understand our life learning tasks and that guidance programs at present are too narrowly conceived. As long as the old indoctrinations worked and the range of intentional learnings remained modest, the deficit was tolerable. But as intentional learning expands, we need better orientation.

Orientation can be provided to individuals in courses, freshman orientation programs, re-entry programs, or as a separate activity. Such orientation can be provided at community, regional, state, and national levels using the media and institutional communications. We know how to sell products, services, and presidential candidates. We can easily orient ourselves to our new learning tasks once we decide it needs to be done.

2. Link the Institutions in the Learning System

Educators, community leaders, church folk, businesspeople, and media representatives need to meet at local, state, and national levels to develop common understandings, goals, and activities to strengthen the learning system. Economic development efforts offer a prototype, but any institution in the system can convene and launch the process. Each institution has enough power not to fear the domination of others, and this coalition building will be an authentic exercise in cooperation for the common good. Each institution is mired in its own language, myths and icons, so the linkage will take time, but there is no alternative.

3. Sharpen the Personal, Communal, and Economic Goal-Setting Process

Because the megatrend of expanded, explicit goal setting is in sight, the organization and improvement of the process is another high priority. The foundations on which to build in each area have been set, as I have described earlier.

4. Develop Institutional Awareness and Adjustments

Institutions need orientation to the new challenges just as individuals do. They must examine the embedded goals, beliefs, programs, and processes that comprise the present paradigm and challenge them as the excellent corporations have done. Hyperbole may be called for in a consciousness-raising campaign among boards, managers, and staff preoccupied with maintenance functions.

Board members and top managers have the task of organizing a sharper goal-setting process, developing the local system coalition, and managing their institutions' adjustment process. The rest of us working within the institutions need to develop new ways of supporting and serving our clients and each other while assuming expanded learning tasks. The rise of support groups, networking, and mentoring in all institutions demonstrates that this role adjustment is underway already.

5. Devise New Ways to Support Expanded Intentional Learning

If there is any truly frontier activity in the new paradigm, it is expanded intentional learning. We need to invent new approaches. Under the old paradigm with its cognitive emphasis, all we did was add a new course, but what does it mean to add a course on caring, courage, leadership, risk taking, inventiveness, or entrepreneurship?

Life planning approaches suggest some first steps. Explicit assessment of one's current status leads to goal setting and planning actions, which we implement with the guidance and support available. This is a helpful beginning, particularly in those areas where knowledge and skill acquisition are indicated. But in the emotional areas a more experiential approach seems necessary, buttressed by the kind of group and mentor support that is always useful when risks are taken. This requires a great investment in research and development.

6. Adjust to High-Technology Delivery Systems

Just as we need a new learning paradigm to help us reach the high-tech age, we need to exploit high technology to put the new paradigm in place more quickly. Millions of us are doing that now with our personal computers, and we have just begun. In addition to the direct instructional use of the new technologies, two other considerations are worth mentioning.

First, the media, with the help of other institutions, must participate in the consciousness-raising campaign which can take place at local, regional, and national levels. Second, educators need to examine their roles in the software development process. Video and computer software is being developed almost entirely without the involvement of the nation's schools and colleges. Since telecommunications and computer-based learning systems are more total instructional systems than textbooks, educators are in danger of becoming "clerks of the works" unless they become more involved and influential in all aspects of these mediated learning systems.

These strategies are all concrete and practicable and can be pursued at modest cost. Most of the means are at hand; only the understanding and commitment have yet to come.

Conclusion

With this brief exposition of the concepts, trends, and strategies leading us to a new national learning paradigm, we reach the end of Part I.

I have defined the scope, the challenges, and urgency of the new American watershed and then summarized our present capacity to cope with its challenges. Although all institutions show signs of obsolescence, adaptation is underway. The very old, but suddenly new, idea of a human learning system is a framework within which we can begin to meet the big challenges. Five trends leading us to a new learning model and six action plans for hastening its maturity bring us to Part II's more specific applications of the model.

If I am even half right in these descriptions and judgements, we have a rare opportunity to "get ourselves together" and create better lives for us all in a very short time.

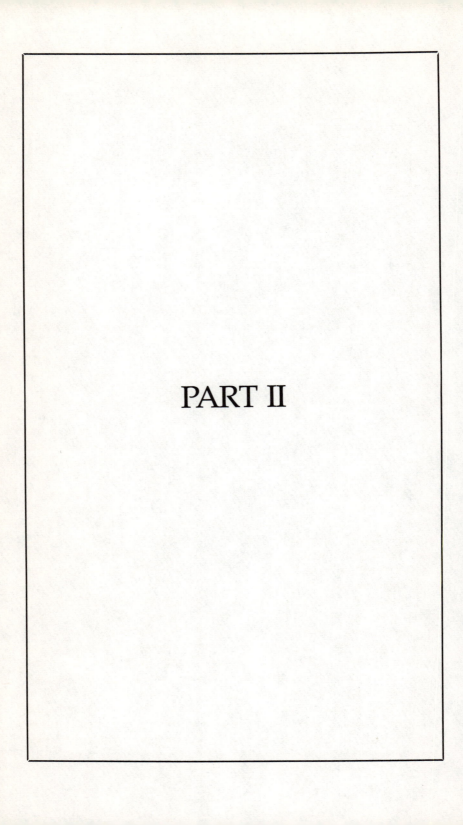

PART II

I turn now from the argument for a new learning paradigm to the strategies and tactics of bringing it to life. The insights of Kuhn and Drucker and all of the planned and managed change of the last few decades argue that we can do better in devising our own future than any generation in history. Strong talk, Niebuhr, but is it really possible or is it another silly tilting at windmills? Recognizing all of the difficulties of personal, institutional, or system change, we have plenty of examples to show that change is possible at all of these levels provided there are the understanding and will.

With the necessary understanding emerging, how do we generate the will to accelerate the process? My father's stories of my Mennonite forebears building an economy and a community in the Russian Ukraine gave me an optimistic belief that institution, community, and nation building are possible and have led me to many interesting but high risk change projects, demonstrating the power of an early indoctrination. The will to risk and try to make a vision come alive was evident in the millions of black and white Americans who participated in the civil rights movement and in the millions of women who shed their second class indoctrinations and in the 600,000 entrepreneurs who started up new businesses in 1982.

So Part II will be concerned with the attempt to bring the human learning system to life. First I will briefly describe the work that a few colleagues and I undertook to get the idea moving and implemented in a few pilot projects. Then a series of chapters will explore the application of the model in our personal and family lives and in all of the mainstream institutions. It might have been more prudent to delay this book until much more implementation experience was available, but this is the moment in our national life when the hunt for a strengthened learning process is underway. The very paucity of experience leaves much room for others to pick up the ideas and invent the future in their lives, institutions, and communities. It could be useful and a lot of fun.

Now That We Have an Idea, What Do We Do with It?

As one reads about the birth of an idea, its diffusion into our consciousness and then into our personal and institutional behavior, the process
seems fairly rational and replicable. Looking back on the evolution of
the industrial age learning paradigm, the new psychology, Keynesian
economic thought, or any other new idea, big or small, we can see how
each new paradigm inevitably replaced the earlier and now obsolete
body of thought and practice. But if you search beneath the overview
to see what really happened, the story is different, full of false starts,
confusion, and conflict. Let me share some of my experiences in trying
to move from idea to action.

As I related in Chapter One, the sources of the idea were both
personal and institutional. Like many of the Great Society warriors, at
the end of the sixties I felt slightly defeated and suffered a profound
lack of closure. We had a sound vision and good support, but we fell
short. As my daughters reached adulthood I began to see the flaws in
their life learning process and worried about the development of my
yet-to-come grandchildren. From my work I began to comprehend the
deepening crisis of American higher education.

An Unlikely Coalition
Is Born

The Delaware Valley Regional Planning Council for Higher Education
was the first setting in which the new learning paradigm took shape.
The DVRPCHE (just try to pronounce that acronym) was the creature
of the seventy-nine colleges and universities in the Philadelphia region.
It hadn't planned much but was a great vehicle for fighting off the
initiatives of the State Department of Education to exert more control
over the institutions. As my late friend and mentor Ed Gates, then
president of Beaver College, quipped, "We are a negative force for
good."

Recognizing that our region would have 40–50 percent fewer eighteen year olds by the mid-nineties and that we were entering a period
of fierce inter-institutional competition for students, some of us wondered whether we ought not to try to expand the adult market for all
of our institutions through a collective effort. So at the Council's January
1976 annual meeting my boss, Marvin Wachman, then president of
Temple University, at my urging made the motion that set up a task
force on continuing education to explore the possibilities. Sister Ann
Marie Durst, then president of Rosemont College, was named chair-

man. In time the planning process was supported by a grant of $146,000 from the W. K. Kellogg Foundation, which has a fifty-year record of promoting adult and continuing education.

Durst is one of those rare people in higher education who really believes in planning, and she structured a process which helped us come up with both a creative plan and a foundation of inter-institutional trust and cooperation. Burying our suspicions, we set about organizing a consortium of area colleges and universities to implement the plan. By 1978 we had completed our work, Sister Ann left for law school, and Clarence Moll, then president of Widener University, became our chairman.

Let me pause to underline the importance of the building of a shared vision and the bonds that develop in key people across institutional boundaries to bring a vision to life. In addition to the small group of presidents that made up the task force, people like Peter Mills, then at the Philadelphia College of Science and Textiles, Gene Kray at the Delaware County Community College, and Ron Watts, then at Cheney State College, began to divert some creative energies to a common cause. Watts's paper on emerging learning needs was heading in the same direction as my own thinking and reinforced our intention to go beyond conventional practice.

By late 1979 the Kellogg Foundation awarded us a grant of $758,000 to operationalize the plan, and in 1980 the task force, now renamed CLEO, the Compact for Lifelong Educational Opportunities, opened its doors.

CLEO's initial program was modest enough. It provided information on the offerings of all member colleges, provided educational and career counseling, assessed prior learning for conversion into academic credit, and conducted a series of staff and faculty development activities. But CLEO also served as the incubator and disseminator of the new learning paradigm and in time augmented its basic services with cutting-edge programs in telecommunications, business services, and the emerging life planning methodology. Its executive director, Lois Lamdin, has a remarkable capacity to move ideas into action. Through its dissemination activities CLEO has developed a national reputation and has generated hope that higher education can build a positive future. More on CLEO later.

The Faculty Decides to Redesign the University

About the time the work that led to CLEO began, I was staffing a newly formed and highly politicized Commission on the Future at Temple

University. One of its tasks was to conduct an institutional self-study as part of the decennial reaccreditation process in higher education. We produced a venturesome report which the Visiting Review Team accepted and promptly went back to business-as-usual; almost none of our recommendations were implemented.

The one recommendation that seemed to have a chance had to do with a planning process that would link board, administration, faculty, and students in a more organized development process. A few of us at the administrative level set to work with friendly faculty then leading the Faculty Senate. It was a rare moment, as faculty-administration animosities are more deeply ingrained than those between management and labor in any smokestack industry. Moreover, university administrators are rarely robust leaders because they are selected by search committees dominated by faculty who believe administration's role is to be compliant to faculty needs and wishes. But even in this idiosyncratic sociology we tried to make the cooperative model work. Within a year we were undone when a dean, dead set against effective university governance, destroyed the effort.

Without an organized process to engage the deepening crisis confronting the University, the Board of Trustees grew restive about its financial condition and in late 1978 mandated a three-year break-even budget and directed the administration to draw up implementing plans. By this time there was clear evidence of the downturn in enrollment, leaving several colleges overstaffed. Bob Schellenberger, a professor of management on leave to the administration, and I organized the staff work to lay out the alternative courses of action. Our conclusion was that the board's mandate would indeed require retrenchment of tenured faculty members, but, even worse, that if nothing else were done to engage the crisis, such retrenchment would be only the first of many retrenchment moves over the next two decades as the supply of eighteen year olds continued to dwindle.

We urged that the University tighten its belt in the short run but that concurrently we undertake the renewal of the University to meet the new needs identified by the new learning paradigm. We laid out a good news-bad news scenario and thought we had been persuasive. As the moment of truth arrived in the summer of 1979, our superiors decided to go only with the bad news part of the plan, that out of a retrenchment strategy we would emerge "tougher and leaner." As the principal advocate of the renewal strategy I had lost the battle. As the University erupted with the news of retrenchment, my colleagues, through some mysterious logic, were angry at me.

Some six months later I received a visit from the leaders of the local AAUP Chapter, the Temple faculty union. Having heard that I had been working on an alternative to retrenchment strategy, an alternative that aimed at preserving jobs, the union leadership wanted to hear more. They responded by setting up a task force to explore the strategy. At its first meeting the task force decided to move beyond its union sponsorship and become a university-wide ad hoc group; they called themselves the Faculty Seminar and in time attracted the interests of over seventy senior faculty.

Fairly quickly the Faculty Seminar came to see the need for a fundamental renewal of the University and set its sights on obtaining a grant to stimulate such activity, undertook an orientation program to persuade their colleagues that retrenchment was not inevitable, and began to communicate their vision to faculty in other institutions. It was a courageous and politically shrewd approach, but then five ex-heads of the Faculty Senate were among its members.

One of the central contributors to the thinking of the Faculty Seminar was Bob Schwoebel, a professor of history and then head of the Center for Contemporary Studies. Bob and his colleagues were in the process of inventing the Gateway Seminar, which sought to overcome the barriers confronting many adults in pursuing their education and to help adults structure a life plan and learning agenda. It achieved these goals by providing an understanding of the scope and nature of change in American society, offering a career and life planning experience, and then providing guidance and continuing support in the implementation of the plan. It was offered to University employees at first so that they could more effectively exploit their tuition benefits and has since been offered in a variety of settings and formats.

The central insight from the Gateway Seminar experience was that most of us do not have an adequately developed learning agenda, the condition of unengaged freedom discussed in Chapters Two and Three. Therefore the need to help learners of all ages to assemble an explicit life plan and an implementing learning agenda became a foundation concept in the proposals being assembled by the Faculty Seminar. As the program development continued during 1981 and 1982, the group also produced a thirty-minute videotape, *A New University for a New Century*, which we distributed throughout the country.

It is the conventional wisdom among college and university administrators that faculty are rigid and unwilling to change. Hence why bother to try? Yet the experience of the Temple University Faculty Seminar shows that the conventional wisdom is wrong. Faculty can challenge their fundamental assumptions, decide that they have grown obsolete, and come to new understandings and commitments to the learning process.

More on the Faculty Seminar later. . . .

Let's Get the New Paradigm
in Place by 1990!

With CLEO and the Faculty Seminar getting underway I began to think about a more systematic approach to the dissemination of the learning system model to higher education and the other institutions in the system. The last shift in the learning paradigm took forty years; why not accelerate the megatrends and achieve it by the end of the decade? My experiences during the sixties taught me that new ideas can move very quickly in the right climate. With education moribund at the time and with the challenges becoming defined, it was easy to predict the critical reports of 1983.

The approach called for an institutional, regional, state, and national dissemination effort. At each of these levels I began an outreach to key people in the institutions of the learning system. The object was to find kindred spirits ready to challenge the conventional wisdom in their own domains and to put some energy into organizing a change process in their institutions or in coalition with others.

If Proctor and Gamble were undertaking this kind of marketing effort quite a few million dollars would be set aside to do it right. The new AT&T is spending fifty million dollars on logo promotion alone. All I had at the outset was my own commitment, a little time, a modest travel budget from Kellogg, a willingness to speak to any audience anywhere, and the ability to write quickly. Clearly I was becoming a zealot, but they go with paradigm shifts.

So from 1980 to the present I've sought to implement this approach by speaking to several hundred groups and writing about twenty articles—really tracts—to educational, religious, business, media, and other groups. As the subsequent chapters will reveal, this outreach has won me many new friends, and I guess some enemies, in the various domains. As one launches forth on this sort of undertaking the fear that it's all a quixotic adventure looms large. I began to feel that we might just pull it off at the 1980 annual meeting of the National University Continuing Education Association (NUCEA), the professional organization of the continuing education deans. Floyd Fischer of Penn State and one of the top leaders in the field had arranged for me to be the convention's keynote speaker, and Kellogg's Arlon Elser invited me to speak to a breakfast meeting of the up-and-coming leaders. There I met Quentin Gessner of Nebraska, Phil Nowlen of Chicago, and Milt Stern of the University of California at Berkeley, all of whom agreed that the American learning system needed strengthening and all of whom have been creative and energetic allies since. I also met Ken Young, the highly respected NUCEA executive, and Adelle Robertson, who had worked with me during her doctorate and who presently leads NUCEA. Their response and subsequent commitment were a turning point for me. While this level of detail is tangential to the argument of this book, it tells a little of how ideas are communicated, accepted, and then acted on.

Part II now begins with a series of chapters on the possible application of the learning system paradigm to individuals, families, and the mainstream institutions of American society: higher education, schools, the church, business, media, and the human services. Since we are only at the beginning, I invite you to join the process and help design our future.

CHAPTER 4

The Challenge of Personal Development

Individuals Are Facing New Tasks

What does the new learning paradigm say to us as individuals? How do we approach the building of our lives differently than we did yesterday? No cadre of professionals is available to provide the understanding and guidance we now need. We can find good career guidance. We can rid ourselves of an ancient fear or other irrational learning through behavior modification. Experts can tell us how to dress for success, become more assertive, manage our time better, be better parents, improve our sexual performance, and so forth. But guidance on how to integrate our desires and goals, how to get it all together and keep it together, is in short supply.

If you followed the instructions in Chapter One, you probably have a better understanding of all your learnings and the many settings in which they were learned. For those personal competencies, traits, and characteristics of which you are proud, I hope you understand which were indoctrinations and which you learned intentionally. In some cases we ourselves were responsible; in some we have someone else to thank. The sources of counterproductive or even destructive personal traits are also important to discover.

In considering earlier learning systems, you have begun to understand the big changes that have occurred in the learning process over the generations. As the old certainties have become more provisional and each of us at any age faces more freedom and choice, what are your current sources of enlightenment and support? The writings of Toffler, Naisbett, or Sheehy, or plays and movies such as *Same Time Next Year*, may have modified our world view and heightened our awareness of change. Women may refer to Betty Friedan and other feminist commentary as sources of insight into changing sex-linked roles. Self-help books provide a ready supply of advice for every new fashion in living, be it open marriages, being "Number One," or having slimmer thighs. Talk-show psychologists and columnists grind out an ever increasing flow of information and advice. Magazines like *Glamour* feed new insights and guidance to their readers.

Each of us is surrounded by this growing array of life guidance services, and much of it is very useful. It helps us set goals and assumes that we are seeking new knowledge and skills intentionally. All of it assumes that we must become more self-directed. These support services have eased the passage from the age of indoctrination but have not given us a new framework for the task of life building which needs to come next.

Back-to-Basics Revisited

We can approach the new life building framework by asking the basic question once again: What do we need to learn in order to meet our life goals? We find the answer by going beyond the early life survival and acculturation learning and explicit curricula of school and college to include role, value, motivational, attitudinal, aesthetic, and emotional learning that are now in the intentional learning agenda. We might even include some of the patterning learning implied by left/right brain research and pursued by new philosophers of the mind. But clearly this learning needs to be put into some sort of a framework that provides for balance and coherence.

One of my former teachers and a pioneer Gestalt psychologist, Kurt Goldstein, discovered an aspect of this need in some brain-injured patients. Unable to structure their physical environment, they lost their sense of coherence and clung desperately to the walls of their rooms as they edged their way around. About twenty years ago the sensory deprivation experiments put people where they could neither see, hear, smell, nor touch. With no environmental input, they became incoherent and drifted into timeless, free floating, disconnected thoughts, images, and feelings.

Most societies have provided for structure, coherence, and balance through indoctrinating mechanisms, though these sometimes created their own problems. In Victorian England the upper classes had so cluttered the heads of their young with parochial rules of living that the liberal arts education provided by Oxford and Cambridge was necessary to broaden their perspective with other viewpoints.

But if the old embedded framework is slipping away, we must either resurrect the old indoctrinations and retreat from freedom and choice or construct a new approach. Most of us have been working on the problem without an explicit framework, magic word, or phrase, but it might make it easier if we had one.

A Theory of Living

In Chapter Two we defined the reasonably consistent framework that we human beings establish for our values, goals, imperatives, role definitions, and the actions instrumental to them as a "theory of living," a term I prefer to "personality" or "lifestyle." Daniel Yankelovich's *New Rules* provides us with the most useful analysis currently available for guiding us in the construction of sound theories of living.

Yankelovich summarizes the vast cultural shifts of the postwar years as the shift from the old indoctrination-based ethic of self-denial to one of self-fulfillment. The old ethic was essential in periods of economic scarcity and useful in an age of economic development. But while it was essential to the production side of the economy, providing hard workers tolerant of difficult working conditions, it was counter-productive to the consumption side of the economy. The success of modern capitalism, with its high levels of consumption, depended on an expanded ethic of self-fulfillment which the new psychology was concurrently developing. This ethic crested in the late sixties, fueled by a burgeoning economy, a consumer-promoting media, and the human potential movement.

The old rules not only sustained the economy; they provided the sense of obligation and responsibility vital to family and community as well. Ultimately the ethic of self-denial brought respectability, self-esteem, and a sense of success. The ethic also tolerated excesses and made for worker exploitation, racism, and sexism, but it provided most of us with a theory of living which brought coherence and balance to our lives.

The self-fulfillment ethic led us astray for a while. We thought the problem of running a successful economy was solved forever and devoted our attention elsewhere. For a time we confused needs with desires and saw self-fulfillment as equal to satisfying the infinite range of desires. Yankelovich describes a young couple to whom "self-fulfillment means having a career *and* marriage *and* children *and* sexual freedom *and* autonomy *and* being liberal *and* having money *and* choosing nonconformity *and* insisting on social justice *and* enjoying city living *and* country life *and* simplicity *and* graciousness *and* reading *and* good friends *and* travel *and* on and on. All are seen as needs they are morally obliged to fill."

Yankelovich goes on to show that the aberration of seeking personal fulfillment in "me-ism" and rampant self-indulgence has begun to pass. It narrows the range of life gratifications in its exclusion of commitment to others, and the economic facts of life now require that we organize an economic transformation. But this does not mean that we will return to self-denial. Yankelovich suggests that we are moving toward a new "ethic of commitment" in which self-fulfillment can be found in deeper and more caring relationships and in common tasks.

He identifies two steps that we must take for this ethic to take hold. First, each of us must move beyond the narrow pursuit of personal desires and see self-fulfillment in the context "of commitments that endure over long periods of time and that the expressive and sacred can only be realized through a web of shared meanings. . . ." Second, he reminds us that such shared meanings are not arrived at by each of us in isolation. Just as the learning system institutions reinforced the self-denial ethic, so must they now reinforce the new ethic with clear and continuing signals. Yankelovich calls for an end to the "anarchy" of institutions and a return to shared purposes.

Answering Aunt Minnie

Until the new ethic of commitment and the new learning paradigm are in place, we need to be more self-conscious about examining and constructing our theories of living. Our experience in the Gateway Seminars and other life planning programs shows such programs can help. But there are no experts, and the field is wide open.

As a start it is useful to give ourselves a context for the effort by remembering that we live in a society with some elemental functions that we carry out in increasingly complex ways. To give us a historical perspective, we should remember that every society has had economic, communal-political, and personal-familial functions, and from earliest times we have always been inventive in executing them and in adapting to changing structures and conditions.

Recognizing the scope and the pace of the change we contend with in carrying out elemental functions is important too. A wealth of commentators, such as Toffler, Naisbett, Etzioni, Will, and Yankelovich, have contributed on this subject. Daniel Bell and Robert Nisbet, who have written over the past three decades on the state of American society, are helpful, as are Frederick Lewis Allen's *Only Yesterday, Since Yesterday*, and *The Big Change*, charming and entertaining recent histories.

Within this context of adaptation to change you can return to the question: What do individuals have to learn in order to meet social and personal goals? Pick up your list from Chapter One and categorize your life learnings. Your list contains many competencies from your intellectual and skill development. It also contains role learning that leads you to define yourself as man or woman, parent, relative, citizen, Baptist or Episcopalian, Italian or German-American, friend, New Yorker or Iowan. That part is fun because you begin to see Yankelovich's point of your connectedness to a variety of groups and people, past and present. Role learning perhaps is best defined in terms of economic tasks. We pay much attention to our occupations and status in the workplace, which is probably why we often introduce ourselves at parties in terms of: Hello, I'm Tom Brown, accountant, engineer, physicist, president of the company, and so forth.

The list of learnings includes a category we call values. If you ranked a list of words that included family, love, success, independence, health, money, religion, friends, leisure, work, etc., you'd have a crude measure of your values. These are key guides for action and self-definition, but we rarely examine and renew them openly.

The list also includes attitudes, motivational patterns, and the emotional or affective shadings of our behavior. Most of these are bottom-of-the-iceberg learnings, and we tend to be somewhat oblivious to them. But they are important aspects of each of us. To dramatize the range of this learning, just look at what comes out of half of the A section in the dictionary: abrasive, abrupt, abusive, acerbic, acquiescent, adept, adoring, adventurous, affected, affectionate, aggressive, altruistic, ambitious, amiable, amoral, amusing, anarchic, antipathetic, anxious, appealing. We didn't even reach caring, courage, cowardice, much less wisdom.

Now if you look at your list and the categories of your learnings, a pattern begins to appear. It is your partly explicit, partly embedded theory of living. It defines you and your actions in various settings. It probably is fairly consistent, although elements of conflict will appear. The pattern may be sufficient to give you a sense of personal coherence, although we can all think back on times of stress and change when we lost that sense. Your theory of living also will reflect your age. Adolescents and senior citizens worry about independence; the rest of us who have it, don't. The notion of life stages becomes a useful contextual tool as we become more explicit about our lives.

As your theory of living sharpens and clarifies, the issue now becomes its adequacy to withstand the current watershed pressures and to guide you to what you will be "when you grow up."

Assessing Your Theory of Living and Setting Goals

Now that the pieces of your theory of living are exposed, they can be rearranged in a sharper pattern. Start with the values, such as success, love, independence, and religious commitment. Then see how they apply to your goals. When I was young, success meant making money, social acceptance and position, and a stable family life. Love was marriage with clearly defined sex roles. Independence meant financial security. Religious commitment meant believing in a particular doctrine, practicing its imperatives, and attending church. We may still use the same value terms today, but we can apply them to a wider range of possible goals.

Examine your values for consistency, and see if there is a hierarchy of values and therefore goals. Most of us will notice that the career and leisure goals are sharper than those for family, community, and religion. Now compare your values and goals with those of your parents; most likely theirs are simpler and sharper. The relative ambiguity of yours measures the loss of old indoctrinations and your failure to take full advantage of new freedom and choice.

Now look at your life roles and see how instrumental they are to values and goals. Also notice the variation in definition. Do the same for affective characteristics. What you are doing is beginning to apply a new level of critical consciousness to your life, putting it out on the table to examine, to evaluate, and to sharpen goal setting. Most of us apply that kind of critical consciousness in our intellectual activity, especially in our work, as we explicitly strengthen our corporate culture, implement a marketing program, or reshape a production process. We are only beginning to learn how to do this in the rest of our lives.

Most people who have gone through the preceding exercise are surprised and delighted that there is more to them than they had imagined. Also, they are somewhat chagrined with the ancient truth that their self-image does not exactly match reality. Gilding the lily is as old as the species. There is always an "espoused theory of action" and the "theory-in-being." Schon and Argyris have explored this discrepancy in their work on the professions. Most people sense that they are deeply connected to others and to our culture. Once they understand their theory of living, they discover that they can do something to improve it.

Let me remind you that taking charge of our lives is just another in a long sequence of developments. The new psychology led us partly down the road, but we had to define ourselves as "sick" or having a "problem" before we were eligible for the ministrations of the new authorities: the psychiatrists, psychologists, and other therapists. During this period we were too intimidated to take charge of our lives. This changed with the advent of the self-help movement, but that tended to deal with the bits and pieces. We have come a long way.

Life Theory Report Card

Now that you have your theory of living before you, the next step is to examine it and challenge its adequacy. We have been expanding this sort of judging for the past twenty years: The civil rights movement led millions of blacks and whites to reject the racist notion of second class citizenship and to excise it; the women's movement made millions of women examine and revise their embedded theories of living. Many of us now question our careers, marriages, and life goals and make other arrangements. And we have only just started.

You can now rate the pieces of your theory. But as you do, remember that you will probably overemphasize the assessment of career. Spend some time measuring your neighborliness and citizenship, and don't forget to evaluate your level of courage or cowardice.

As you complete the assessment, you'll better understand your own personal learning system and how it led to your present theory of living. You'll begin to have a better sense of why we need to strengthen the system. Most importantly, your assessment will inspire you to action.

Upgrading a Theory of Living Through a Self-Contract

After you have assessed where you are, the next step is to decide where you want to be. We are skilled in career planning, and now we can apply those methods to other dimensions of life. Recall that more explicit goal setting is a key megatrend leading us to the new learning paradigm.

The ritual of New Year's resolutions is a useful background for upgrading a theory of living. Utopian goal setting is worse than a waste of time, ensuring failure and making goal setting harder the next time. Goals of any kind need to be achievable within a reasonable time frame. In the Gateway Seminar we ask people to set a short-term goal and implement it. Surprisingly few people have experienced setting and attaining goals, and many are pleased to find they can do it.

Some examples of short-term goals resulting in successes were: A woman who was in a car accident and lost her driving confidence won it back; a young man who was always late handing in assignments broke the habit; many lost weight or exercised more; and one woman made Christmas presents for a handful of nieces and nephews. These may not be exciting examples, but they reinforce the process, and most big, long-term goals can be broken down into short-term pieces like these.

We found it also helps to share the process with others. A good friend, a small circle of friends, or a life planning group at a local community college can help cut self-deception, increase the realism of the goals, and provide helpful suggestions and valuable support. There are some good ideas from a growing pile of books on the subject, such as Dick Bolles's *What Color Is Your Parachute* or his *Three Boxes of Life*.

The goal setting should lead to a written contract with yourself, complete with an implementation plan. We've adapted the life planning process for college students and now suggest a six-year time frame to be sure that the goals extend beyond college. But the time frame is up to you, depending on the goals you set. The contract, however, must be comprehensive and must include goals in those areas that have been at the bottom of the iceberg all this time.

In the present cultural climate, career goals, and action plans tend to dominate life planning groups, but other life changes take place concurrently. The almost uniform discovery is that we have a greater capacity to enhance our lives than we ever imagined. As a result our self-esteem rises and we feel wonderfully empowered. As the nation looks for reinvigorated economic productivity it need look no further than the undeveloped human potential of its people.

CHAPTER 5

Families and Other Intimate Arrangements

The Family Has Been Through Change

Most of us have a good sense of what has happened in our family lives over the past two decades. From direct experience, observing others, reading, and media watching, we know we've been through a revolution. For those of us over fifty who lived most of our lives under the "old rules," the scope of the change is astounding. Those of us who married, set up households, and started our families during the 1950s would not have believed the current acceptance by most Americans of premarital sex, working women, remaining single, remaining childless, unmarried mothering, interracial marriage, living together while unmarried, and sharing household and parenting responsibilities. But it is estimated that only 20 percent of our population still believe and enforce the "old rules."

A rich new vein of historical scholarship is beginning to augment our understanding of *what* has happened with a better understanding of *why*. Philippe Ariès's *Centuries of Childhood*, first published in the United States in 1965, describes the many forms family life and childhood have taken. In a relatively short time our belief that the family is the natural site for meeting biological and social needs has been undermined. The counterbelief that the family is shaped by a variety of cultural and economic influences and therefore is subject to more intentional intervention has grown accordingly.

Christopher Lasch's *Haven in a Heartless World* documents what he calls the "invasion" of the modern family and its functions by the agents of the new psychology, the welfare system, etc. More recently Jacques Donzelot's *The Policing of Families* describes how the emerging professions of medicine, education, and psychology, out of a misplaced idealism, have worked to "police" the concept and functions of the modern family. The picture that emerges is similar to that of the school: Too much is expected from one institution. When it fails to deliver, we intervene and disrupt it further.

Any of us who started families in the 1950s will recall how professionals of that era "policed" our concept of marriage and family life in a friendly but insistent manner. But within the decade the model was ridiculed by the counterculture and the feminist movement and rejected in favor of alternatives which promised to provide more self-fulfillment. Now that the excesses of that era have run their course and the craving for togetherness is reasserting itself, how shall family and other intimate arrangements be redefined? We could develop a new orthodoxy with new "policemen" to enforce it; in 1983 a rash of new family books appeared to do just that. Brigette and Peter Berger's *The War Over The Family* restates the importance of the family and suggests ways to strengthen it.

The results of the 1983 *Better Homes and Gardens* magazine survey of American family life provide a more promising direction. Eighty percent of the 200,000 readers who responded agreed that the American family was in trouble, but the vast majority said that with a lot of hard work, they were successful in keeping their own families productive and together.

These families have accepted change and have been working to establish the "new rules" Yankelovich calls for. Without a new orthodoxy to guide them, they show greater tolerance and acceptance of freedom and choice for themselves and their children. The operation of two of the learning paradigm megatrends can be inferred from the survey results: Successful families are involved in sharper goal setting and are more self-directed. They are engaging their freedom and choice in positive, adaptive, and responsible ways. (Also, of course, successful families are more apt to answer voluntary surveys.)

Family Is Only One Part of a Successful and Balanced Life

Three truths should be stated about the vast cultural drama we are living through. First, construction of a productive family life must be seen in the context of other life tasks and other sources of satisfaction. We do need to run an economy, we do need to run our communities, and we need some space for our personal lives. The family "policemen" of the fifties made me feel guilty over the time and energy I gave to my work and my community interests. The human potential "policemen" of the sixties took away my obligation to family, work, and community and insisted that my only obligation was to myself. Now there are no dominant social enforcers, and it is up to each of us to shape our family lives and put them in context with everything else that we want to accomplish. The issue of balancing family with other life tasks needs to be pursued more explicitly than ever before.

Children Need an Extended Period Of Nurturance and Protection

A few years ago a *New Yorker* cartoon depicted a middle-aged man in mod clothes saying to a child, "Don't call me Grandpa, call me Bernie." The loss of the old indoctrinations has taken away the clear inter-generational role distinctions between grandparents, parents, and the kids. Marie Winn's *Children Without Childhood* documents the loss of innocence and protection from the adult world and the growing exposure and participation in it. This sobering account shows this loss of innocence as an inadvertent by-product of all the other cultural shifts of the past two decades. Winn argues that this is no way to raise children, and I sense that the parents who answered the magazine survey feel likewise. A three year old is not an adult, and an extended period of nurturance and protection needs to be built into family life.

In *An Immodest Agenda* Amatai Etzioni concludes that increasing numbers of families fail to provide their children with the foundation of learning prerequisite to success in school. The loss of family instructional time and energy to competing demands of working parents, parental self-centeredness, and television probably has as much to do with the decline of academic performance as any school deficiencies. This is exacerbated in underclass communities where single-parent families face inordinate challenges of making ends meet, fighting off the competing pressure of the peer group, and making a life where the odds of success are very long. Trying to motivate a youngster to achieve in neighborhoods where more than 80 percent of young people are unemployed may be an impossible task.

The Quality of Family Life Depends on the Quality of the Community and the Economy

A third truth is that the quality of family life depends on the quality of our communal and economic lives. As the new psychology moved us inward, both in our personal and family lives, we neglected to maintain safe and caring communities. But such communities are essential to the larger tasks of personal development, reinforcing the family in the parenting process. Growing up in my East Harlem neighborhood, I was surrounded by a lively culture which was rich in do's and don'ts, caring and protection, and street drama, funny and sad. Growing up in a suburban community on a quarter-acre lot, my children were deprived of the richness of such a culture.

The recent recession has reminded us that unemployment has an adverse effect on family life. The rise in wife and child abuse as a consequence of the indignity of losing one's job must be seen as an economic cost. While we seek a return to personal responsibility, we cannot return to blaming the victim. Unless the economy can produce jobs for all who need and wish to work, both for their own support and the maintenance of their self-esteem, we will undermine our culture. We have been doing this for forty years with the welfare system and by not providing work for young people, whose self-esteem is most vulnerable. I would guess that the dramatic rise in teen-age suicide is linked to unemployment.

A growing number of dislocated workers, mostly blue-collar men, sit at home while their wives work. If the transformed economy can be successful without full or even reasonably full employment, how do we maintain self-esteem and family life for the millions of people on the shelf? Given this context, how might the new learning paradigm help us in engaging the new freedoms and choices of constructing our family lives or whatever arrangements we make in living with our "significant others?" There are some directions, if no panacea.

The Need for a Critical Consciousness

The critical consciousness we are now applying to our personal development needs to be extended to constructing our family lives and other intimate arrangements. Clearly we are exercising new choices in our more varied living arrangements, a high rate of divorce, and open homosexuality, but we are only partially aware of the tasks of family building. How do we orient ourselves; how do we orient children and young people to the expanded scope of their life learning tasks?

Talk-show psychologists, magazines, and self-help books do only a partial job. Do we assign the task of providing family guidance to some new institution or profession? Do we try to resuscitate an old institution or profession? Since we are taking charge of our lives, we are not likely to do either. The solution is not to provide the answer for people but rather to sharpen the question and then provide them with the means of arriving at their own answers.

We are setting new economic goals and specifying related learning tasks; we must do the same for family issues. The conservative political agenda includes the strengthening of family life, but the rhetoric has not led to action. It may be they don't know how to intervene. Indoctrination is not the government's business, but it is a political obligation to call on the rest of us to get on with all of the life learning tasks.

Parents, for example, need the kind of information Marie Winn's book offers. My guess is parents are not treating children as adults intentionally; once they realize the need to structure an extended period of childhood, they will do so. Moreover, as they come to recognize the advantages of structuring their own life learning agenda more explicitly and intentionally, they can help their children do the same.

As we begin to form coalitions to strengthen local learning systems and answer public questions related to economic and community development, the critical consciousness of the citizens of their personal and family development tasks needs to be engaged as well. To avoid inadvertently reestablishing indoctrination modes, such coalitions need to link to community and neighborhood institutions such as PTAs which affect people on a daily basis. The re-creation of community to ensure that we live in safe and caring neighborhoods relates directly to the strengthening of family and child development. Again, the first step is to ask what kind of family life we want; once the question comes into sharper focus, we can then set about providing the answers for ourselves.

Birth Control Is Just One Part of Family Planning

If young couples are writing marriage contracts and specifying goals and responsibilities for one another, if we are setting goals more explicitly for ourselves, and if the excellent companies are designing explicit corporate cultures, why can't the notion of family planning be extended beyond birth control to other dimensions of family life?

Elements of such intentional goal setting have been increasing in number for some time. Not satisfied with our own indoctrinations, my generation turned to Dr. Spock and other gurus to learn how to be proper parents. Spock happily anticipated an increase in self-directedness and advised doing what felt right. We have sought out information on nutrition, exercise, and drug and alcohol use as we take more responsibility for maintaining our health. The feminist movement has introduced new modes of goal setting in sex-linked roles, and clearly women are ahead of men in this respect. Betty Friedan and other feminist writers are beginning to explore the family strengthening issue, but we still have a long way to go.

The New Technology Also Influences Families

One of Landon Jones's key points in *Great Expectations* is that the very size of the post-World War II generation disproportionately impacted American culture. We heard a lot about self-fulfillment, energetic hedonism, and sexuality as that generation moved through their twenties. Now in their thirties, the emphasis has shifted to commitment and the search for continuing sources of support in networks, friendship, and stable relationships. As this generation matures we may be able to look forward to a series of quiet inventions in the better structuring of family life with greater tolerance, respect, sharing, and responsibility for one another.

The task is more difficult for that generation than mine. With more and more women working, the competing demands of jobs and other obligations make balancing roles and responsibilities harder. Constructing more explicit family plans entailing firm commitments of time for sharing, as well as for developing new routines and rituals wherein this occurs, must take a high priority. Millions of us may soon be able to work at home for a good part of the workweek, communicating through our home computers. Many families can stay closer to each other than the old nine-to-five pattern allowed. But projections suggest that this development will impact only 10 to 15 percent of the workforce.

The home computer may have other benefits as well. Active family sharing through computer games seems an improvement over passive television viewing. Perhaps we can generate a new kind of software that allows for shared activity among siblings, parents, grandparents, and friends to counter the possibility of further isolation caused by personal computer work. As we speculate about these developments, the task of ensuring that they apply across class and income lines looms large. The new consciousness and technologies so far have divided class and income groups more than they have brought them together.

Conclusion

Of all the watershed issues, I am least optimistic about the challenge of strengthening family life. The loss of indoctrinations and the rise of competing demands from career and recreational interests have tilted the balance away from the family for many of us. Despite the conservative rhetoric, our institutions and the media send fewer messages about the family challenge than about the others. As we create learning coalitions to review the state of life learning in our communities, I hope that the family issue comes into focus at least as sharply as the economic issue.

CHAPTER 6

A Memo to Politicians

The Need for User-Friendly Politics

I am more positive about politics and politicians than most people I know, having come to consciousness during one of the most exciting and vital political periods in this century. My earliest political memories are of listening to Roosevelt's "Fireside Chats" and New York Mayor La Guardia's Sunday radio programs. If Roosevel played the calming and reassuring leader during the Great Depression, Mayor La Guardia, our "Little Flower," amused and reassured us at the same time. He was our protector against the excesses of corporate power who read us the comics when the papers were on strike. Given that kind of leadership and its human presence in the neighborhood political storefront clubs, politics was more "user friendly" in those days.

Considerable debate about repairing the depression-frayed economy prevailed during my college days. Many of my professors were engaged in political activities and were excellent role models for my generation, which became very active politically. Our student political groups were superficially cynical, but we felt an idealism and sense of possibility that I don't think have been matched since.

When I came to Philadelphia in 1950, a political renaissance matching the La Guardia era was taking shape. The level of civic excitement and participation was thrilling. Many of us so lost touch with reality that we thought Adlai Stevenson would win the presidential election in 1952.

I mention these early and very feeling-laden experiences because politics and politicians can be so central to our own sense of personal and communal identity and well-being, especially in times of crisis. About the only "highs" we experience these days are when our team wins the World Series or the Super Bowl. Then it is we who have done the impossible and become "Number One, Hi Mom," not our team's highly paid professional athletes.

Politics are a demanding business, and we have been lucky that some men and women can tolerate the grinding campaigning and still have time and energy to master the issues. Good politicians are quintessential lifelong learners. They are not entirely self-directed, since politics define the issues. Other people usually define the problem or need and move it to the political stage, and still others develop and promote the solution before the good and smart politician gets into the act. *Ministers of Reform*, Robert M. Crunden's recent book about the Progressive era that began a century ago, might give us some perspective as we meet our current challenges.

Progressives Had a Moral Vision of a Good Society

Like today, an economic transformation was underway during the Progressive era, leading to the mass industrial economy and an urbanized nation. As we've seen, the learning system of that time needed strengthening, and the necessary changes were made. But the quality of life was in jeopardy; the moral sensibilities and institutional practices adequate for an earlier age were no longer satisfactory. A generation of thoughtful men and women restated the moral vision of their religious heritage in secular terms and gave the nation what Crunden calls a "civil religion of American mission." Jane Addams, John Dewey, George Herbert Mead, and their followers laid the foundation for a spate of innovations and inventions in education, health, the arts, religion, and politics. Most importantly, they helped create a social agenda so that some of the surplus from the burgeoning economy was directed to parks, museums, libraries, hospitals, and the infrastructures in transportation, roads, water, and sanitary systems so essential to decent urban life.

The Progressive political inventions included the initiative, referendum and recall, and a commitment to strengthened local and state government. Theodore Roosevelt and Woodrow Wilson brought an interventionist stance to the federal government that continued until Ronald Reagan came into office.

The economic transformation of that time was seen in the context of a moral vision of a "good society." The politics of that time were built on that vision. We are in the early stages of a similar economic transformation but are as yet without the context of a moral vision of what the "good life" or the "good society" ought to be.

Etzioni, Will, Yankelovich, and Naisbett serve in the same early warning role that the Progressives did a century ago. They all see economic transformation in the cultural and personal development context, and it is time for our politicians to do likewise.

The Search for a New Political Agenda

It is no secret that political parties as broad-spectrum aggregations of like-minded people have been in trouble for some time. We seem to manage only personality or single-issue politics at the moment. As an old knee-jerk New York liberal Democrat, I sense the loss of political identity deeply and wish it were otherwise. If only I could have the faith of the New Rightists, in terms of my own values, of course. The old liberal agenda has been met for the most part, though some of its solutions are defective. Is it sensible to consider creating a new political agenda around which the party structure can be built, or must we continue playing the current special interests, single issue game?

I do know that the watershed issues will have profound political consequences. Fundamental issues centering on rights and responsibilities, definitions of equity, justice, liberty versus equality, and communal control versus personal choice will all surface in new forms.

Presidents Carter and Reagan have been sensitive to our present condition in very different ways. As I was struggling with the learning system concept and trying to define my sense of the watershed, President Carter sought the counsel of citizens and cultural commentators to find out what needed doing and how to reshape his administration to do it. This anticipated Naisbett's "participatory democracy" megatrend. The product, the "malaise" speech that followed, fell short, and the president's obvious groping for transforming political agenda terminated. Though the effort failed, Carter should be given great credit for the courage to conduct the process openly.

President Reagan also sees the nation at the watershed. His sense of the causes and remedies are different, but he is on target in believing that family, community, personal responsibility, and other nongovernmental institutions and processes must be strengthened for the nation to prosper. My major complaint is that the rhetoric on these aspects has not been matched by any significant action. The implementing strategies explored in the next chapters require no new federal agencies or expenditures, so he or the next president will be able to match words with deeds.

The search for the new political agenda continues, with the 1984 presidential campaign providing a marvelous opportunity to orient the citizenry to the scope of the new American watershed and what we all must do to meet its challenges. Once we understand the challenges we can debate some of the economic issues such as industrial policy, but the challenges of personal development and re-creating community haven't been recognized yet. If we again build a constituency only by seeking to assemble all of the single-issue groups in a big enough mosaic to win the election, we'll miss the opportunity for citizen orientation.

The search for a new political agenda will fail until we develop a new framework of understanding from which specific agenda items will flow. In watershed periods obsolete institutions are incapable of providing this new framework. But with their litmus-paper sensitivity to new issues and emerging realities, politicians tend to be ahead of everyone else, and they become the lead "teachers" of us all. Many are trying to do just that, and I urge them to escalate the effort to bring all of the watershed issues out in the open and speed us toward the next political agenda so that we can renew our sense of the "good society" and the "good life."

Practical Political Policies

Any politician responding favorably to this book would want to move quickly toward practical applications. This is why the thrust of most national reports is on specific remedies like the length of the school day and year, competencies to be learned, merit pay for teacher, and so forth. My suggestions build from the six strategies outlined in Chapter Two.

Orienting the Citizen Learner: Every politician is continually speaking on issues. Armed with sophisticated opinion poll data, they are careful to tailor their views to their constituents' concerns; hence politicians follow rather than lead the voters. In reasonably stable times this is sound practice, but when great change is needed, it isn't. K. Patricia Cross, a thoughtful analyst of shifting trends in education, provides a compelling example of such a situation. If a poll asking people about their need to preserve perishable food in the summertime had been conducted in 1910, most respondents would have asked for better ice, cheaper ice, or better insulated iceboxes. They would not have mentioned refrigerators, which had not yet been invented.

Similarly, a politician's speech should center on three points: The nation is in a watershed period facing the primary challenges of transforming the economy, renewing community, and strengthening personal development; we are inadequately prepared to engage the watershed ("the nation is at risk" would grab attention); and we must understand the megatrends already bringing us to the future and accelerate them by making the necessary adjustments in ourselves and in our institutions. After a little embellishment appropriate to the locale and the audience, I'd suggest that we all decide to set the necessary goals, from heavily decentralized to regional and local levels, agree to meet them by 1990, and then close with a Kennedy-like, "ask not what your country can do for you, but what you can do for your country" and be ready for a standing ovation!

Part of the orientation game plan could include friendly competition, since competitiveness is a national characteristic. Each city, county, and state could be encouraged to compare itself to others on a scale for economic and communal renewal. As we've learned from *In Search of Excellence*, the smart companies hand out many awards and rewards, with amazing results.

Linking the Institutions in the Learning System: All politicians, candidates and elected officials, can help orient the people. But those in executive positions can take the lead in bringing learning system institutions together to arrive at some common understandings and goals. Eventually educators at all levels should become the continuing leaders of such an effort, but political leaders already concerned about education don't have to be pushed far to reach the new learning paradigm.

Because governors, mayors, and county executives have access to the right people, they can assemble "doer" groups quickly from schools, higher education, business, media, churches, civic agencies, and other relevant institutions and give the project a running start. Unlike the economic area, where goal setting is easy and implementation is expensive, this goal requires little in terms of resources, physical facilities, or external support, and every community, city, region, and state has the intrinsic ingredients required to strengthen its learning system.

Sharpening the Goal-Setting Process: Once the learning coalition is in place, one of its principal tasks is to set goals. It won't get far unless all constituencies achieve a "back-to-basics" orientation so that they move past the present learning paradigm and delve more deeply into the "what do we need to learn in order to achieve our goals" question. Asking each member to go through the learning iceberg exercise might help everyone remove the professional masks they wear.

Once the group participants understand the range of learning required to run their own lives, they'll better understand what's required to run an effective community or productive economy. Then the group might assess its list as you did in Chapter Four, only focusing on the community this time. As they begin to talk about the quality and condition of the county, city, region, or state, everyone will have views on crime, health, family stability, and all the other indices of communal life. Some may have partial data, but no one is likely to have a comprehensive data base for such indices.

Earlier I mentioned the work of Community Leadership Seminars in Philadelphia and the long-range planning review we were conducting. We decided that we were wasting valuable time at the seminars by requiring our speakers to give the student-leaders the pertinent data. We concluded that it made sense to develop a fact book on Philadelphia. Soon we became conscious that the civic leadership needed such a "snapshot" of Philadelphia as a base for its leadership; all Philadelphians could use something like this to comprehend their city and build more effective citizenship.

In exploring the data sources for such a picture, we found many fragmented data bases but no one comprehensive source. CLS and the Center for Philadelphia Studies at the University of Pennsylvania are now assembling such a base in order to continue assessment and sharper goal setting. Every local learning coalition can do this, share the results widely, then communicate the data to the public in an annual event in which "Podunk takes a look at itself and sets new goals for next year's civic agenda." The newspapers can publish such a piece as an annual supplement, and local television stations can help promote it.

The trend to sharper communal goal setting has rippled through the nation for some time now. Those of us who worry about such matters in Philadelphia are envious of Minneapolis which has institutionalized an effective goal-setting process. A number of resources are available there to provide technical assistance and others' experience. The National Community Education Association, the Domestic Policy Association begun by David Matthews of the Kettering Foundation, the Public Agenda Foundation started by Cyrus Vance and Daniel Yankelovich, and the Council for the Advancement of Citizenship are some key resources.

Short-term goals which can build confidence in the process should be set at the start. Increasing computer literacy is an example. Few inventions have moved into our lives as quickly as the computer, and it has just begun to affect us. A basic tool in our economy's transformation, it is changing communications with electronic mail, data transmission, and data base access for learners of all ages. The "electronic cottage" is already a reality for many of us. The promotion of computer literacy is spreading into the nation's schools and colleges as a basic skill. Why not take it another step and make this a community or regional goal? Adults need computer literacy too, and with the help of newspapers, radio, and television as well as the computer industry, such a concrete short-term goal could generate others. A new computer literacy course now available through PBS could be the center of such an effort.

Every city and state has a complex array of goals, but many if not most are indistinct and implicit. Once they are more explicit and realistic, citizens can be involved in their implementation.

Developing Institutional Awareness and Adjustments: Politicians can contribute to the institutional adjustments required by the new learning paradigm in three different ways. First, they can orient the public along with institutions to the need for building learning coalitions and defining goals. Every institution will be under pressure to rethink its structure and process, and politicians can keep the heat on.

Second, the legislative process can be employed to speed these changes. With the exception of the church, the structure and process of all mainstream institutions and professions have been affected by legislation. Hundreds of categorical programs maintained by the federal government contribute to the fragmentation of the institutions and professions. Once in place they tend to stay that way, but the annual budget and reauthorization process is an opportunity for stimulating institutional awareness and adjustments.

For example, long discussions on updating the 1934 Federal Communications Act so far have failed to acknowledge the media's key role in the learning system. Shouldn't we criticize the media along with the schools? The Vocational Education and Higher Education Acts are up for reauthorization, providing an opportunity for Congress to help these sectors of education renew their functions in the context of a strengthened learning system.

Third, the message of *In Search of Excellence* can be applied to government, with explicit strategies like those developed by business. Government leaders may have less flexibility than chief executive officers, but they must set an example of change for other institutions.

Devising New Ways to Support Expanded Intentional Learning: Moving some of the bottom-of-the-iceberg learning into an intentional learning mode is an important challenge of the new model. This strategy will take some research and development investment. Just as politicians are ready to support R&D investment in better math and computer literacy teaching, they now need to push for better ways to learn "entrepreneurship," "inventiveness," and all of the other affective learning instrumental to a transformed economy and a "good society." This is probably the most important area in which to push back our ignorance.

Effective politicians can also stir people's emotions and call for courage, compassion, and other feelings necessary to meet goals, solve problems, or face crises.

At the federal level some agencies such as the National Institute of Education, the National Institute of Mental Health, and the Fund for the Improvement of Post-Secondary Education could be asked to develop a research and development agenda. There is a chain of regional education research labs and centers that could pitch in.

Adjusting to High-Technology Delivery Systems: As we've all seen in recent years and will continue to see throughout the eighties, the adaptation of the new technologies into new learning delivery systems is moving us into a post-Gutenberg era. The first of two key political tasks is to put pressure on the schools and higher education to adjust, and the second is to protect the public's interest in these developments. Millions of dollars' worth of educational computer software will be sold during the next few years. A consumer advisory service sponsored by the school system or local community college would be valuable. The reservation of adequate channels for public purposes is a major issue as cable systems and satellite-based distribution systems develop. The present climate of deregulation could shortchange the public unless some safeguards are established.

The new American watershed and our need to strengthen the learning system are real opportunities for our politics and politicians. With most other institutions struggling for perspective, those of you sensitive to change can provide it and lead us toward a new political agenda and a vital period in American politics.

CHAPTER 7

Renewing American Higher Education

The Demographic Crisis

During my third career as a university planner in the 1970s I began to explore the developing crisis facing my institution and all higher education. This led me to explore the national learning process, to visualize how we might strengthen it, and to spend five years in zealous advocacy for change. I am optimistic—hopeful that with some understanding, leadership, inventiveness, and energy we will meet our challenges.

Higher education faces three very severe pressures in the 1980s, but it is aware only of the first: fewer students. After a century of success, including three incredible postwar decades of growth, the prospects suddenly are bleak. Currently about 3,000 colleges and universities spend approximately seventy billion dollars each year educating close to twelve million full- and part-time students. Before we became familiar with the demographic realities, particularly the fact that post-World War II children were not reproducing themselves, college administrators were planning for straight-line expansion of the student body right into the twenty-first century. At Temple we thought we needed to plan for a student body of 70,000. Temple in 1983 managed to enroll about 33,000 students, having suffered a drop of more than 15 percent so far.

Actually, by the mid-nineties the nation will have 26 percent fewer eighteen year olds. The Northeast, Middle-Atlantic, and Mid-West industrial states will average a 40 percent decline, while the sunbelt states will drop 15 percent. Philadelphia County, where I live and work, will experience a 50 percent decline, and we have seventy-nine degree-granting institutions in the region!

The ripples of the demographic certainties are severe. First, the loss of tuition income and the related public subsidies deepen an already painful economic crunch. Second, and more disturbing, any attempt to cut back staff and faculty, typically by seniority, accelerates the average age of those remaining to sixty by 1990. While we all plan to be intellectually vital at that age, an intellectual community needs to nourish its roots with bright young scientists and scholars to retain its creative and critical vitality. Two decades of retrenchment is hardly a positive strategy to cope with this demographic dip.

The best that the higher education leadership has been able to manage is to accept this retrenchment scenario as the only way to the future. For example, the Carnegie Council on Policy Studies in Higher Education's final report, *Three Thousand Futures*, gives no alternative. After twenty years of generating exhaustive reports on the subject, the council and its predecessor Carnegie Commission, both under the chairmanship of Clark Kerr, former president of the University of California, can only say, "Well, friends, these are the facts. Wish you lots of luck!" A parallel report from the American Association of University Professors, the major higher education faculty organization, concurs with Kerr's council that continuing retrenchment is the only future possible.

Competition in the Education Business

The second pressure higher education faces is the loss of its monopoly position. Other institutions such as libraries, museums, schools, professional associations, and corporations are moving into the education business. The latter began training and educating employees during the past few decades because higher education was not interested in providing those services. Some estimate that forty-six million Americans participate in an organized educational experience every year. Only twelve million, or roughly one-quarter, attend a college or university for such service. Also, new technologies are spawning new for-profit educational enterprises which are and will be challenging higher education institutions for the adult market.

Allen Tough of the Ontario Institute in Educational Studies called our attention to the fact that most of us are agents of our own learning in a variety of ways. An abundance of learning materials in the self-help sections of libraries and book stores, or even in hardware and building supply stores, suggests what's available. The personal computer promises a quantum leap in such learning. The present textbook market for both kindergarten through twelfth grade and higher education is about a half billion dollars a year; the educational computer market projected for the late 1980s is between four and six billion! Much if not most of these products will be purchased by parents or self-directed learners. We'll no longer be dependent on any one institution for learning.

A Silly Season

The pressures of demographic decline and new competition from other education providers are the two most visible parts of higher education's deepening crisis. But the third, the question of institutional legitimacy, is more elusive.

No more than ten or fifteen years ago higher education could do no wrong. But somewhere in the mid-sixties public support began to erode. Some questioned our management of the rebellious student movement; others felt we had oversold our capacity to solve the nation's problems through research, which had led to heavy government investment. These factors do not fully explain the gradual fall from grace, however.

In the pre-Civil War era the nation's colleges lost touch with our changing learning needs, were held up for ridicule, and remained in the national doghouse until the new land grant institution and urban colleges arrived with an educational model more responsive to the needs of the rapidly developing mass industrial society. It could be that once again we have lost touch and need to rethink the model.

Bob Craig, vice-president of the American Society for Training and Development, confirms this judgement. He suggests that higher education must be in a "silly season;" with so many new learning needs being identified, all higher education leadership can think about is two decades of retrenchment!

There are new learning markets, new sources of income, and renewed legitimacy for those who remove the blinders. But if the nation's house of intellect seems blind to the changing realities, it should be recognized that a college or university is a conservative organization surrounded by professional, disciplinary, accrediting, and a wide range of governmental organizations, each of which pushes for standards within the present model but which resists change outside that model. it sees itself more as the keeper of the cultural heritage than as a catalyst for change.

When the new land grant or urban college came into existence in the last quarter of the nineteenth century, it was staffed heavily by faculty from existing colleges with commitments to earlier educational points of view. As Lawrence Veysey points out in *The Emergence of the*

American University, there was great debate during those formative years among advocates of the British-born liberal learning ideal, the research ideal newly arrived from Germany, and the new American idea of utilitarianism. The debate never came to closure, however, and left America's public university without a coherent point of view. As soon as the new institution became successful, largely because of its evangelical fervor in taking practical knowledge to rural America, there were enough resources for each group to retreat to its own academic pigeonhole and nourish its ideal in isolation from the other two. The debate never resumed, and the problem of academic leadership grew difficult if not impossible. University presidents needed to be acceptable to each faction; therefore the model of the successful president became the mediator-conciliator, and so it remains to the present day.

The Penn Central Question

Part of the problem is that we've never adequately asked and answered the Penn Central question. At the time of Penn Central Railroad's demise, the most telling criticism was that it had not adequately probed the nature of its business. Was the company in the passenger- and freight-hauling business via trains or in the transportation business? The answer made a difference.

For higher education the question would be: Is it in the course, credit, and degree business or the human learning business? Higher education's failure to apply to itself the magnificent intellectual qualities evident in so many diverse scientific and scholarly areas is paradoxical. Again, this failure stems from the premature closure of that debate on mission and purpose. Instead of struggling to integrate the liberal learning, research, and utilitarian perspectives into a coherent and synergistic whole, the early success of the new institution shut off the debate, and we were left with three relatively unrelated cultures in our universities.

Although the utilitarian function was the basis of higher education renewal in the early twentieth century, from the end of World War I until the present this function has been eroding, losing status and prestige along the way. Ask any continuing educator of any college or university about acceptance and status within the academic community, and you will hear what life in the back of the bus is like. In today's retrenchment climate, it is often continuing educators who feel the ax first. Because they are an institution's best hope for new markets, sources of income, and sensitivity to emerging learning needs, the axing seems less a prudent cost-saving move than institutional self-immolation.

Community Colleges Are
Taking the Lead

Despite all that is wrong with our colleges and universities I find no area of national life wherein our inventiveness has been greater than higher education. It has fueled the economy, enhanced our artistic and public lives, and enriched our personal and family lives as well. But the vision and evangelism so compelling in the early decades of this century have dimmed for all but the community colleges who now are our best hope.

The two-year junior or community college has existed since the turn of the century, and from the late 1950s on has developed and expanded rapidly. Its rise coincided with two pressing needs. When the first demographic bulge of post-World War II babies reached college age, they overwhelmed existing four-year colleges and universities. Inexpensive local institutions from which graduates could transfer were welcome. The two-year colleges also met local manpower training needs, especially for those who were not going on to a baccalaureate degree but who needed to learn a technical or para-professional skill.

At one point there was a new community college opening its doors at the rate of one a week. Now 1,230 of them educate close to half of all college students. Community colleges find themselves at the bottom of the academic pecking order, along with continuing educators, but they, like the corporate educators, are closer to understanding and meeting the emerging learning needs of the nation. They will lead American higher education by 1990.

The Mission of Higher Education

Our present answer to the Penn Central question contends that higher education's essential job is to teach, conduct research, and provide service, a definition which does not set goals but lists instrumental activities. A better definition argues that the mission is to develop, transmit, and apply knowledge, but even that definition restricts learning to the cognitive top-of-the-iceberg level. This was generally adequate for most of the twentieth century, but it institutionalized the separation of the humanists, scientists, and utilitarians.

For me the mission of the nation's colleges and universities is to participate in two fundamental societal processes: the development of people and the improvement of society's structures and processes through the intellectual work of the faculty. Higher education is linked to the larger learning system and can bring attention to the changing needs of people and institutions. This definition avoids the ivory-tower image and makes it possible for higher education to play a leadership and guidance role.

But what are the chances of renewing higher education's vision and developing a strategy considering the new market and income requirements necessitated by the decline of the eighteen year olds? Despite the fact that twenty years of retrenchment of tenured faculty and staff will diminish vitality when it's needed most, the chances of change are much better than I would have thought several years ago. The business and political pressures are a godsend!

Some Signs of Hope

The real question is whether higher education can be the agent of its own reform and renewal or whether they will be imposed from the outside. Some evidence of capacity for self-improvement is appearing within this generally defensive and demoralized community:

- Many institutions are beginning to reach out to the adult market. In doing so they have to recognize and adjust to the changing learning needs and different learning styles of adults.

- Many universities are becoming aware of the economic trans-formation's scope and their potential role in it. In Pennsylva-nia, Governor Thornburgh has created the Benjamin Franklin Partnership in which business and higher education coalitions are accelerating economic development on a regional scale.

- Steven Muller, president of Johns Hopkins University and leader in higher education, has addressed the issue, suggesting that during the next decade there will be more change than in the past hundred years in who is educated, what they will learn, and where and how they will be educated.

- Boards of trustees are becoming restive. The Association of Governing Boards prepared a special report on the new higher education environment to help orient concerned trustees. Since many trustees are also business leaders who understand the scope of the economic transformation and its human resource implications, it is not surprising that they would begin to worry about the response of the colleges and universities on whose boards they sit.

- In the summer of 1982 Quentin Gessner, continuing education dean at the University of Nebraska, Lincoln and president of the National University Continuing Education Association (NUCEA), convened the Association's leadership group for two days to reach consensus on a renewal agenda for continuing educators. That consensus, based on the learning system concept and strategies, founded a yearlong effort to inspire the membership with a new vision and role, and its effects have rippled out to many settings around the country.

- That same summer the board and staff of the W. K. Kellogg Foundation completed a major review of their priorities. They concluded that the nation needed more than anything else a fundamental improvement in the adult learning process. Guided by Chairman Russell Mawby, President Bob Sparks, and Program Director Arlon Elser, the Foundation has positioned itself as a leader in bringing a new learning paradigm to life, much as the Ford Foundation did twenty years ago in the Great Society programs. I can't emphasize too strongly the importance of our national foundations in stimulating the change process.

- That fall a very important Lifelong Learning Leader's Retreat was convened by the American Association of Adult and Continuing Education (AAACE), led by Wendell Smith, continuing education dean at the University of Missouri, St. Louis and the Association's immediate past president. The retreat brought together the leaders of twenty national associations that affect adult learning in some way and asked them to discuss the current situation and devise ways to deal with it. As a consultant to the retreat I was not hopeful, having seen other such meetings fall short of their goals.

  This one was different. World-weary and cynical though they may be, these people are sensitive, and they arrived knowing that they faced a fast changing environment requiring a new order of response. By the end of the second day there was an air of excitement as new ideas and evangelism began to build. The nation needed a new lifelong learning policy and commitment, and we educators were to lead the public to its continuing learning tasks.

  The retreat's ultimate success lies in the follow-through process, and already several important steps have been taken.

The idea of campaigning for a strengthened learning system in the same way that candidates and products are sold to the public was born at this meeting. After several months of preliminary exploration Bob Craig, representing the corporate educators of the American Society for Training and Development; Quentin Gessner and Wendell Smith, representing AAACE and NUCEA; Dale Parnell, representing the community colleges; and I met in Battle Creek to design the campaign and present it to Kellogg for their guidance and support. This book is a result, and several other steps of the campaign are now underway.

- During 1983 Dale Parnell, president of the American Association of Community and Junior Colleges, initiated a process within the AACJC Executive Committee and Board to update the community college model. This is the first example of a major sector of higher education, representing 1,230 institutions and educating 4.9 million students, taking a hard look at itself and producing a new strategic plan and vision. It is a great act of responsible leadership which I hope will stimulate the other sectors to halt retrenchment and begin work on the new learning paradigm.

- The tasks required to bring a new paradigm to life include recognizing its urgency. They require allies and prototype projects, supportive foundations, and a research and development mechanism to keep refining and improving the ideas and their application. Twenty years ago the Great Society programs lacked this and the initial ideas were implemented before they were ready, wasting billions of dollars and, even worse, betraying the hopes of millions of Americans.

Happily an initiative by NUCEA to strengthen its members' professional development began to broaden its scope to the larger research and development function. Alan Knox of the University of Wisconsin, whose *Adult Development and Learning* is an early version of the learning system concept, is leading the NUCEA project to bring the critical balance to the campaign. Perhaps we can do better this time.

These illustrations provide hope for higher education as the agent of its own reform. During our visit to the Kellogg Foundation, our hosts wondered why the nation's great universities were not providing new visions and bold leadership. We answered that change typically begins at the edges, rarely at the center, and that community colleges, continuing educators, and corporate educators are showing the way.

Recognizing that such leadership is beginning to develop momentum, let us consider again the six implementing strategies and their applications to higher education.

The How Tos

Orienting the Citizen Learner

After achieving understanding of the scope of the new American watershed and the learning paradigm's emerging shape, any professor, guidance counselor, academic department, college or university, consortium of such institutions at local, regional, state, and national levels, and any coalition of national associations can undertake the orientation of the nation's learners to the expanding tasks of their lifelong learning agenda. There are advantages of scale, but anyone can begin the orientation process tomorrow. Twelve million students in 3,000 colleges and universities together could send out the messages about as fast as the 1982 Tylenol story.

Individual faculty members can model such an orientation on the work done by the Temple Faculty Seminar, exemplified by Judi Stoyle's integration of a life planning component in Temple's Introduction to Business course. A more ambitious example is seen at Wilmington College, Delaware, where Ron Watts, a pioneer of the Compact for Lifelong Educational Opportunities, has arranged to have all entering students sharpen their learning agendas in the context of the new challenges.

The CLEO project is working on a regional orientation effort in the Delaware Valley in collaboration with other institutions in the regional learning system. Regions can be defined by the signal area of local radio and television stations, which can feed new orientation messages to the public effectively and economically.

Our national campaign seeks to approach national, state, and regional citizen orientation by providing materials, prototypes, and technical assistance to interested parties at any level. Politicians can start it, the higher education community can guide follow-through implementation, and other institutions can contribute to the synergistic process.

As we enter the turbulent part of the paradigm shift, I would expect the new orientation to life learning to be built into family, community, and church life and into the media and schools. By the end of the decade both young and mature adults will arrive at colleges and universities with a much clearer idea of what they want to learn.

Linking the Institutions
in the Learning System

In the immediate future political leaders can beat the drums and convene institutions within the presently fragmented learning system, but in the long term the leadership role of building and maintaining local, regional, and state learning systems is open to higher education. In the early decades of this century higher education led the cause through extension services and outreach to families, youth, communities, and local economies, and this must be done again.

Higher education's network of relationships with schools, business, the cultural community, human services, civic organizations, etc., exists now, but for narrow purposes. We almost returned to expanding the purposes fifteen years ago with the idea of "urban extension," and the idea has surfaced again as we try to improve technical assistance to small and mid-size businesses. Dale Parnell is pushing hard for community colleges to take the lead in urban extension, and we may see some useful prototypes in the next few years.

The approach is very simple. Once the watershed challenges are understood and higher education accepts that life learning occurs in many settings, local learning coalitions can be developed to stimulate an improved goal-setting process. Doing this requires pulling the right people together, developing shared understandings of new or restated goals, and adjusting accordingly.

We have been trying to do this in Philadelphia through CLEO, but it takes time to interest the right people, and it's easier in a smaller community. An interesting prototype is now developing in southeastern Pennsylvania under the leadership of Dick DeCosmo, president of Delaware County Community College. After DeCosmo and his staff drew up a list of key people in business, government, schools, and religious and civic communities, we then went to visit them to explain the new learning paradigm. The group agreed that Delaware County needed a strengthened learning process to reach a better future, and all agreed to participate in forming a county-wide learning coalition.

Sharpening the Goal-Setting
Process

Higher education can help in the goal-sharpening process on three levels. First, it can become involved with other institutions in setting economic and communal goals. Many connections already exist, but the goal-setting process is mushy or nonexistent. In the case of De-Cosmo's initiative in Delaware County, the economic goal setting is in pretty good shape, largely due to the creation of the Delaware County Partnership, a coalition put together by the County Commissioners. The communal goals vary by local community but nowhere reach the scope required. A community college can be enormously useful in providing leadership for community agreement on common goals and providing the data base necessary for assessment and subsequent goal setting. Any local college or university has the talent necessary to support this process once they accept it as part of their mission.

Second, higher education can help with individuals, as described in Chapter Four. It can begin with its own students to gain experience and improve the process and then move on to help other institutions and the public at large. Although we have made good progress in the life planning process, it's still only suitable for individuals and small groups. The Educational Testing Service (ETS) and several other groups have developed first-generation computer software useful for career and life planning. ETS's System of Interactive Guidance and Instruction (SIGI) helps individuals clarify values and build a career development theory and implementation plan. With the large-scale move to personal computers, the need and market for such software will expand, and higher education ought to take a lead in developing these materials.

Third, higher education ought to be sharpening its goal setting in terms of its own programs. It is generally agreed that despite the individual excellence of many teachers, courses, and programs, the aggregate curriculum has lost its coherence. My argument is that the curriculum never had much coherence, but as long as students brought their own it didn't much matter. Now that students are enrolling with inadequate bottom-of-the-iceberg learnings, colleges and universities have a new problem. Subject matter alone does not comprise a curriculum.

Higher education, like most of elementary and secondary education, has been confusing ends with means. Because it is hard to specify the ends, performance goals, competencies, and other "output" criteria, we have tended to measure quality through "inputs": the number of PhDs on the faculty, books in the library, square feet per student, or credit hours accumulated per degree awarded. Military and corporate education and training have been able to specify performance goals to evaluate their efforts, but higher education has not.

A few years ago Ken Young, now NUCEA executive director, was the head of the Council for Post-Secondary Accreditation (COPA) and oversaw the organization and implementation of a major study of the input-dominated accreditation process. It recommended shifting to output-based evaluation and accreditation, but Young reports that very little has happened. Competency-based education became an issue in the seventies but largely failed. Ruth Nickse of Boston University has managed to take that corner of adult basic education programs dealing with high-school equivalency and convert it to a performance- compe- tency- output-based system.

The problem is that we do not ask the basic question: What do we need to learn to meet our disparate goals? Thus we fail to identify either the goals of learning or what's needed to reach them. Once we define the goals we can define the competencies required.

Since we have spent much of the present century avoiding the value judgements and commitments basic to setting goals in the per- sonal, communal, and even the economic areas, colleges and univer- sities are going to have to move past the prevailing value relativity and begin to engage the issues of the "good society" and the "good life" as Walter Lippmann, and Cardinal Newman a century earlier, expect us to do. This clearly doesn't mean we have to go back to Victorian England and have a rule for every possible situation, but it does mean that we need to move through a long delayed value clarification exercise and decide what we stand for.

Developing Institutional Awareness and Adjustments

Four key activities are needed to implement this strategy.

First, American higher education needs to stop thinking about its present structures and processes as God given and eternal and begin to see them as part of a learning paradigm that has served the society well but is now obsolete. If it can understand its location in the larger societal learning system and the adjustments required by the new American watershed, higher education can then become part of the solution instead of the problem. Perhaps business pressures, enlight- ened political leadership, and a few inside agitators can accomplish this within the next few years.

Once this recognition takes place, things can begin to happen. Higher education can then begin to help with the institutional aware- ness in the other domains. Keep in mind that since colleges and uni- versities prepare people for almost all of the other institutions, we are as much the keepers of the others' cultures as our own. Therefore we have a special obligation to revise our own institutional awareness quickly so we can help the others, be it K–12 education through our colleges of education, business enterprise through the graduate busi- ness schools, health care through the medical and allied health schools, etc. If the internal goal setting in each of these applied professional programs considered the watershed challenges and the emerging learning paradigm, we would play a truly prophetic role in American life rather than our current anchor-dragging role.

Designing institutional adjustments is the third part. What does a college or university do differently? How does a president redesign his role? What is the changing role of a faculty member?

With a broader understanding of the college or university mission in the adjacent learning system, trustees could be far more active in linking with other domains and setting external goals. Presently they are kept at arms' length, and they could be more effectively utilized.

Presidents face an exciting role adjustment. Presently they are primarily maintenance managers. Faculty members mistakenly believe that they are the academic leaders, but few have a comprehensive sense of the institution. All parties need to accept their inexpertness and adjust. In addition to a new internal leadership role, presidents need to see themselves as leader-guiders of the larger learning system, as many of our evangelical founder-presidents were a century ago.

The real opportunity for faculty is to become whole people again, both intellectually and in a new dimension of working with learners. Left to their own devices for decades now, their fragmentation and the growing remoteness from changing learner needs are totally counterproductive. This was recognized by the Temple Faculty Seminar and needs to be recognized by faculty everywhere. The redesign of reward systems to recognize integrative, innovative, cross-disciplinary, and cross-professional work is a first order of business. The new learning paradigm calls for a rebirth of mentoring in the learner-professor relationship. As the Temple Faculty Seminar discovered after twenty years of doing it the other way, the new paradigm provides new satisfactions and challenges for the middle-aged professor.

As a first step, I'd have all presidents and all faculty read *In Search of Excellence* to exorcise some of the residual anti-business sentiment in academia and to begin to ask if we couldn't learn a little about the construction of an inventive and humane environment from the best companies.

The fourth key activity is inventing new structures within which to conceive and support human learning. The learning system is more a metaphor than an operational structure. But we must incorporate the school, college, media, personal computer, and other parts of the system into a new operational learning structure. Judith Stoyle, Ed Mazze (dean of Temple's School of Business Administration), and I have been working with such a structure, taking a leaf from the Health Maintenance Organization in the health care field. The HMO concept has several advantages: It is a way to shift from illness care to the more positive health maintenance as a value and goal for both persons and professionals; it structures a new delivery system; and it offers a way to pay for the services rendered. Our analogue is the Educational Maintenance Organization, or EMO, as a new structure in which the new learning paradigm can be advocated and delivered. I will have more to say on the EMO idea in Chapter Eleven.

Devising New Ways to Support Expanded Intentional Learning

Our theoretical and applied knowledge is weakest here. Yet each of us as we review our affective competencies and decide that we need a bit more courage or compassion or some additional intimacy and interpersonal competence will be engaging our expanded intentional learning in whatever way is available to us. Unless the mainstream institutions help support such learning, the charlatans surely will. Therefore it is vital that higher education acknowledge these new dimensions of intentional learning, alert the citizenry as to what we know or don't know, and begin an R&D effort that meets the need and protects the public and consumer interest.

Among the creative people working in the area is Arthur Chickering, who published a landmark book in 1981, *The Modern American College*, arguing for an explicitly developmental approach to higher education. He summarized the scientific literature and offered a variety of perspectives on how to apply the knowledge available in a collegiate curriculum.

Adjusting to High-Technology Delivery Systems

Higher education is not holding its own here. In historical terms it has done less with television than it did with radio, and despite what Carnegie Mellon and Drexel Universities have done by incorporating the personal computer in their curricula, higher education is falling behind.

Just as the implementation of the learning system concept requires some new structural inventions like the EMO, so does the challenge of high-technology delivery systems. The present decentralized college and university delivery system with its use of faculty, courses, and textbooks as primary ingredients is ill-equipped to produce the necessary telecommunications and computer software and to organize and operate national or international satellite-linked, interactive delivery systems. The pioneer in high-tech delivery systems is Ron Gordon, Atari's former chief executive officer, who invented the first foreign language phrase computer translator and the first computer delivery system. This links the home computer, phone line, satellite, and instructional materials and resources around the country and the world. More are sure to follow, but none are coming from higher education.

The decentralization of our 3,000 colleges and universities and their further fragmentation into two-year, four-year, public, private, religious, and other categories, compounded by the dominant governance of higher education's public aspects at state rather than federal levels, reinforces the need for new structural inventions. Consider what would have happened if President Kennedy had asked the Joint Chiefs of Staff to coordinate the armed forces for the space program! NASA was necessary, and higher education needs an equivalent organization to protect its stake in high-technology delivery systems.

Thoughtful politicians and business leaders like Ron Gordon and William Norris, whose Control Data Corporation has invested over one billion dollars in the PLATO system of educational software, would see the wisdom of an educational NASA. Otherwise we could be caught in the crossfire of entrepreneurs and educators competing for dominance and profits in the fundamental process of operating America's learning system on which all of us and future generations are dependent.

A Crossroads

Among this book's many messages, one of the most important is that American higher education is at a crossroads. Our nation's colleges and universities are not like Lockheed, Chrysler, or Braniff and cannot be replaced overnight. Caught in an obsolete learning paradigm in the midst of a revolution in human learning, higher education requires rapid transformation. Some of us are trying to do this from the inside, but we welcome all the help we can get from thoughtful allies in the political community, business world, and any other sector that sees human learning as something requiring a long hard look beyond the quarterly, or even the annual, bottom line.

CHAPTER 8

Schools and the Learning System

What Can a Superintendent Do?

A few months ago I was invited to speak at a conference attended mostly by K–12 educators. Although I was eager to speed my message, I decided to pitch it more generally than I typically do to a higher education audience. While I see the new learning paradigm in cradle-to-grave terms and see its implementing strategies stretching across the lifespan, my own work and experience in applying the model have been with young and mature adults. So I tried to ease the pain and defensiveness the national reports had caused and encouraged the educators to see opportunity in the present environment.

I gave them Galbraith's observation about criticism cloaking new aspirations, outlined the watershed challenges, gave the rationale for the new learning paradigm, explained what some of us in higher education were doing, proposed that we learn to work together, encouraged the administrators to see the fun and excitement of strengthening the learning system in their backyard, and sat down. They applauded, we discussed the issues, and I thought I was home free.

During the break a school superintendent asked if I'd join him for a cup of coffee. He complimented me on my work but complained mildly that I hadn't given him many specifics to take home and implement. I tried to get off the hook by saying that I hadn't been deeply involved in K–12 issues for fifteen years, but he'd come a thousand miles and wanted his money's worth, and we settled down for a long conversation.

The superintendent, Jim, told me about his district on the edge of a big city with a touch of suburbs, an old small town, and a remnant

93

of country at the far edge. The suburban piece was more blue-collar than usual because of an adjacent steel mill and had more than a touch of reactionary culture, to Jim's regret. Many "blue-collar kids" were unemployed. The old small town had a black working-class neighborhood and a fringe of garden apartments increasingly populated by single-parent families, mostly headed by working and divorced women. "Latchkey kids" roamed the town streets in the late afternoon. The remnant of country was no problem as children there went to private school.

Jim clearly was on top of educational research literature and was ready always to push innovation. As a principal in the late sixties he had become the district "itch" in pushing equal education programs, working closely with the black leadership. He deplored education's recent decline. He had learned early on that if a school cares and maintains high expectations for all students, they will care too and rise to the expectation. He saw his primary task as finding principals who were strong leaders and who would provide safe and structured environments in which both teachers and students could focus on the essential learning tasks. He knew that classroom teaching was tough and demanding work and insisted that administrators provide the support, nurturance, and respect any committed teacher wants and needs.

Jim sets goals for everything he does. He was an early supporter of competency-based education and hoped it would return. Deeply committed to the present emphasis on incorporating critical thinking and problem solving into the curriculum, he worries about excessive television viewing and has experimented with a program in critical television watching for fourth graders. He agrees that the expansion of intentional learning was a frontier task for American education. Even though Jim tries to stay on top of his field and obviously has great pride in his accomplishments, he has come to feel that the changes and challenges are getting ahead of him.

We reviewed the changes in family life over the last fifteen years and agreed that the expanded freedom and choice represented a gain, but with costs to children. The research seems clear that divorce has a negative effect on learning. We both had just read excerpts from Winn's *Children Without Childhood* and agreed that too many parents were mindlessly extending freedom and choice and dimensions of adulthood to children long before they were ready. Jim agrees with Etzioni's observation that more and more children are coming to first grade without the self-organization and interpersonal skills necessary for successful learning. It was time to bring back a little more structure and perhaps indoctrination for youngsters.

When Jim became an educator, the schools had good community

support from active and vital PTAs and civic organizations. He too had noticed the decline of community spirit and involvement since then, concluding that this was the consequence of the "me-ism" environment and the fact that fewer residents had school-age children. He was intrigued with the notion that the learning system no longer was providing the necessary instruction and reinforcement and that the intentional learning agenda would have to include community responsibility skills as well.

We didn't have to talk much about the economic challenge. He had had his board set up a task force to connect with the local and regional business communities, and his vocational education people were very supportive. He was delighted with the business response and had even made friends with some of the business leaders he had met. I wasn't surprised about this affinity as Jim reminds me of some of the chief executive officers I had read about in *In Search of Excellence*.

I proposed that Jim and I walk through the six implementing strategies as they applied to schools. Maybe I could help him, and I was sure he could help me come up to speed in the K–12 applications of the paradigm.

Orienting the Citizen Learner

The superintendent agreed that the issues of how children understand and act on their life learning tasks was one of the most unexplored areas in American education. A century ago, when the present paradigm was established, parental and school authority was considerably stronger, and the pedagogical assumption was that children would do what they were told. But self-directed learners need to understand the what and why of their own learning. A new and important priority for educators and parents has appeared, and the attention-grabbing power of the watershed metaphor could help them establish a more explicit learning agenda.

Although Jim warmed to the challenge of orienting his total community of 30,000 to the watershed and the new learning tasks, he decided that was the easy part and turned to the children for whom he was immediately responsible. One of his kindergarten teachers pursuing a master's degree in educational psychology had been telling him about "metacognitive" theory, which centers on the development of critical consciousness or understanding what one is doing and why. The teacher had been trying to observe this in five year olds and help them label and understand their life learning tasks, updating Aunt Minnie's question, What are you going to be when you grow up?

Even the very young have an idea of values and life roles. Although

Jim's schools had been working on the career development process for some years with a sequence of program modules at elementary, middle, and high school levels, perhaps it was time to do a similar program for life planning. Maybe the next thing to do was to bring the kindergarten teacher and kindred spirits from the other levels together to conceive of the process in developmental terms and articulate the orientation components at each level.

The notion of the individual life plan that I had described in my talk resonated in Jim's mind. Since he had an exemplary special education program for retarded and developmentally disabled children, he knew all about the Individual Educational Plans, contracts that students make for themselves to achieve certain goals. Why not adapt these to become Individual Learning Plans? He pointed out that parents were as responsible as the schools in supporting such plans, and we agreed that it was time to broaden the planning group to include parents. The school would assume its obligations, the parents theirs, and the students theirs. We would update the contract every year, set annual goals, measure our achievements at the end of the year, and then go through it again.

We had gone past the scope of the first strategy and were moving into others, but it did help sharpen the issues, processes, and actors relevant to the orientation task.

By the time we finished this part, Jim had his plan for further exploration within his schools and with parents and was making a list of key community leaders for the larger community orientation program. At this point I suggested another cup of coffee as we discussed the community orientation issues in the context of the second implementing strategy.

Linking the Institutions in the Learning System

Jim barely gave me time to stir in the sweetener before he was off again. He had always admired Larry Cremin, one educator who always had acknowledged that learning occurs in many settings. Of course parents, communities, churches, peer groups, and media are vital parts of the learning process for good or bad, and of course they ought to work together in support of common goals.

So Jim got out the pad again and listed the small town mayor, the Church of Christ minister, the editor of the local weekly, the president of the county community college, the woman who ran the human resource development programs at the steel mill, and others. He knew all these people well but had never quite seen them as fellow leaders of the local learning system. It reminded us about the story of the child with the ravioli phobia. The psychiatrist was trying to prove that raviolis were harmless and slowly began to assemble one. He pointed out that each ingredient was harmless, and the child agreed. But as the last corner of dough was forked together, the child fell apart. It was now a ravioli, and dangerous.

We agreed that the weekly Rotary luncheon was going to be much more interesting as the newly formed learning coalition started to make its plans to strengthen the local learning system. One of the problems we identified was that of communicating at the level of a school district on the edge of a big city. The big city media, both print and electronic, tend to dominate the suburban ring, making local communication and identity formation difficult. But if the local institutions coordinated their information flow, it might be possible to synergize the impact. Moreover, if the goal setting was an exciting process, the communication problem would take care of itself. I asked Jim about cable television and learned that a thirty-channel system was running, but no one had thought about using it as a public communications mechanism. Certainly, there were unused channels. The pad came out again.

Sharpening the Goal-Setting Process

I asked Jim about the present state of goal setting in his community. The county had established an economic development unit to attract more high-technology business, but it didn't mean much at his community level. Jim's task force was focusing on career and manpower development issues, not job creation or economic development. The big city had its own unit badly coordinated with the surrounding counties. Did it make sense to sharpen economic goal setting at community levels, or should participation take place on a county or regional scale? We came to no conclusion, but we agreed that a community goal-setting process ought to make people aware of their economic roles as worker, consumer, and citizen. It might make Jim's neighbors more creative and effective wherever those roles were played. We talked about the need for enhanced inventiveness and considered that trait a communal as well as personal goal to be pursued.

The present goal-setting process for communal issues wasn't in any better shape. Several civic groups took on projects from time to time, but none were comprehensive or had continuity or dealt with the real quality-of-life issues. I mentioned that the Philadelphia CLS had concluded that we didn't have an adequate set of civic labels or a data base for developing proper assessment and goal-setting processes on a regular basis. I mentioned the possible role of the community college in getting that base together for Jim's area, and he agreed, but he thought some of his high school seniors could also do the job under proper supervision. There were no overriding issues calling for crisis goal setting. However, Jim and others had recognized a slippage in community spirit and involvement over the years, and it seemed time to get a process started.

We already had covered an improved personal goal-setting process as far as students were concerned. For adults, the Church of Christ minister was doing something of the kind, and the local book store seemed to sell quite a few self-help books. Jim recalled that his adult evening school always filled up its five- or ten-session courses on anything dealing with personal and family development. Perhaps it was time to "mainstream" personal goal setting. The weekly paper and cable channels were unused, readily available resources.

All that was left to discuss was the vehicle to focus community attention on the goal-setting process. Jim thought that participating institutions could be brought together in a town meeting which could be broadcast live throughout the community.

Developing Institutional Awareness and Adjustments

Concerning the readiness of his board, staff, and teachers for the new learning paradigm, Jim indicated that there were many complaints about the critical national reports. Some principals were openly angry, feeling their schools were doing fine. They understood the need for economic transformation, and there was much interest in moving along on computer literacy and the math/science fronts. Many complained about declining parent involvement as more mothers worked and no longer could come in during the day. But Jim thought they were ready to listen to a new idea, especially one that countered the bad press education was receiving and one that held out the possibility of becoming a leading school district.

As institutional awareness developed, how would role adjustments be made? Jim laughed, saying he had already rewritten his job description this morning. He was going to delegate much maintenance management and try some bold leadership. He was going to conduct two workshops quickly for the Board of Education and for his principals. He wanted the board to support and push the paradigm actively in the larger community, and he wanted their help in linking with other institutions. He wanted principals to take the paradigm and its rationale to their teachers, parents, and students, demonstrating community as well as educational leadership in the process. Then he'd begin to talk about adjustments with the other institutions in the learning system. Jim had been concerned about the latchkey children and now concluded that local churches should arrange after-school programs. If they were going to expand their role in a strengthened learning system, this would be a good first step.

Jim doubted that the teachers' union would oppose him on any of these plans. They were on the defensive too and could see that rehabilitating the institutional image would be good for everybody, especially at budget time.

Devising New Ways to Support
Expanded Intentional Learning

Jim was quick to pick up my unease and insecurity with this strategy. He had recognized that children were just not learning responsibility as effectively as in the past. He had been thinking about building an "each one teach one" technique into his schools so that older students learned to be responsible for younger students and sharpened their own competencies in the process. Secondly, he knew the information economy would require group competencies and had recognized that, with the exception of athletics, his whole curriculum reinforced individual effort to the detriment of group effort. He had begun to think about building such activities into the curriculum.

Boy Scouts, Girl Scouts, and church activities were possible settings for expanded intentional learning, and Jim reported that the scouting organizations seemed to be thinking similarly. We agreed that the goal-setting process should identify key traits that could be approached more intentionally and that could lead to pilot activities in improving support for their development.

Adjusting to High-Technology
Delivery Systems

Jim knows we are in the high-tech age and that the delivery systems are bound to change. He is prepared to accept the electronic cottage with families taking on more of the learning job. Jim thinks schools ought to become consultants to these families and still be available to provide school-based education for other life learning not best learned at home. As a member of the Computer Alliance organized by the National School Boards Association, he is up to date on the latest computer applications in education. We agreed that the next decade is going to be unsettling as we adjust to the new delivery system, but he felt there was no need to worry. "Just keep your eye on the goals and the means will fall into line," he said.

Beyond "Basics"

Toward the end of our conversation I wondered whether or not we should spend some time on current proposals about a lengthened school day and year, more homework, merit pay, improved teacher preparation, and other issues. Jim found merit in most of them, but he also found it unproductive to focus totally on the schools. Our conversation had reminded him that human learning and productivity have many sources, and he agreed it was essential to improve the schools, but even more necessary to improve the rest of the learning system. I believe there are many people like Jim ready to move on to the new learning paradigm.

CHAPTER 9

The Church and the "People Business"

The Penn Central Question: What Is the Church's Business?

The nation is fortunate in having a creative group of cultural commentators to give it perspective and guidance in this watershed epoch. I have sought to acknowledge my debt to them throughout this book, but I have one particular problem with most of them, as I have with much of modern social science. The abstractions seem more real than the people from whose behavior the abstractions are derived. Social trends, forces, institutions, systems, processes, and so forth are abstract concepts based on the individual and collective behavior of people. I may be nit-picking, but as a practicing change maker I know of no way to move an institution or strengthen a system other than to affect people's heads and hearts and change the way they think, feel, and behave. That is why I have sought to enliven the ideas, concepts, and strategies of the new learning paradigm by connecting them with people.

Finding and making friends with kindred spirits is a by-product of idea peddling. One such new friend is the Reverend Harold Viehman. Now retired, he was the executive director of the United Ministries in Education, an ecumenical effort of a number of Protestant denominations to provide a focal point of inquiry and action on life learning issues. I mention Viehman at the outset for two reasons. His zeal and zest on behalf of his calling remind me that ideas do not live independently of people's believing and acting on them. Also, he helped me understand the modern church's core problem with a remark born of a lifetime of frustration: "We've just got to get the church out of the religion business and back into the people business!" Hence the title of this chapter.

Viehman was betraying no loss of faith. He is no closet agnostic nor secular humanist. The precepts of Christian faith and its theological elaboration are as vital and valid for him at the end of his career as they were at the outset. He actually was asking the Penn Central question: What is the essential business of the church? His answer is people and their nurturance, guidance, and liberation from all of the afflictions and tyrannies known to mankind.

The Declining Influence of the Church

Whether one sees the church as a consequence of divine inspiration or as a marvelous human invention to give us the source of guidance Lippmann talks about, it can be recognized that it has been the primary manager of human learning throughout much of history. Through the ages family and community have drawn their goals and instructional agenda from an ancient alliance with the church. Modern religions, built on earlier world views, laid the foundation for our era. They provided a coherent framework for our understanding of the universe and for the rules of daily living. The church, in league with family, community, and, until recently, government, was the prime agency for indoctrinating the populace in bottom-of-the-iceberg learning, in addition to transmitting premises and imperatives at the cognitive level.

At the same time, the church in its creative and prophetic moments moved beyond its earlier indoctrinations and liberated human consciousness and intellect. It played a primary role in inventing schools and colleges, and the liberal church's moral vision had as much to do with the expansion of freedom and choice as any secular agency. Even today it is still a pivotal learning setting for millions of people.

The impact of the church on my development was more cultural than religious. Because I wasn't Italian or Catholic like my friends in East Harlem, I had to be something, and I searched for heritage and definition throughout my adolescence. There was no Mennonite church in New York at the time, so my parents shipped me off to the First German Baptist Church of East Harlem. The Germans had all moved by then, and I was one of the only residents attending. My parents warned me of the church's mission to baptize at an early age; we Mennonites regarded this as an adult decision and commitment. I became wary and left the church at the age of fourteen.

But the religious impulse hadn't left me entirely, and I almost made it to the clergy. As it happened I met too many Mennonite young men who had escaped life on the farm for seminary in New York. My developing New York cynicism and sophistication were clearly incompatible with these role models, and I looked for other callings. At this time theologian Reinhold Niebuhr had captured the liberal imagination in the church and elsewhere, and I was constantly asked about my relation to him. My initial reply, "Reinhold who?" was hardly adequate for the budding New York savant. I began studying Niebuhr's views on social gospel, which are very compatible with the simpler Mennonite notions of community service, and they added an important dimension to my life learning.

I had been at arms' length from the institutional church for almost forty years and felt just a little tense when it was time to reacquaint myself with what the church people were thinking about human learning and education. I asked Bob James, then in campus ministry at Temple University and a great ally during the hot days of urban crisis in Philadelphia, to introduce me to some of his friends. He organized a lunch where I had a chance to speak with about fifteen people, mostly from other campus ministries, and I met Hal Viehman there.

Through Viehman I met a number of kindred spirits in other denominations and at the National Council of Churches who also were struggling to redefine the role and mission of the church in a stronger learning process. They felt a sense of urgency as it was evident that the authority and influence of the church had been declining throughout this century. Although every denomination had an explicit statement on its support of K–12 and higher education and sought to advance the moral and human concerns of the church in concert with educators, the old sense of coalition was diminished, if not absent, in most parts of the country. Evangelical and fundamentalist denominations retain a more compelling sense of authority over their members, and the Mormons have maintained the most effective integration of religious and educational goals of any church while remaining part of the modern era.

The decline of the liberal church's authority and effectiveness relates to the challenge of the new psychology. The liberal church began to curtail its own indoctrinations to stay current with a modernizing membership but failed to fill the resulting vacuum. Still needing help with our freedom and choice, many of us went elsewhere: to the analyst's couch, to the human potential movement, to self-help literature, and even to cults when the pain of freedom grew too strong. To put it harshly, the liberal church, albeit inadvertently, abandoned its members to the secular professions and institutions.

In spite of this loss of authority and influence, none of the national reports on the educational crisis has identified the church as part of the problem or solution. I am not aware of any significant public commentary by church leaders or organizations in the reports, though a century ago such reticence to discuss educational policy publicly would have been unthinkable. Viehman's frustration is with the institutional church's acceptance of its decline and with its retreat to a narrower "religious" agenda focusing on ritual observance and organizational issues relating to buildings, congregational size, resources, and management.

The liberal church lost its leadership role in the national learning system because, like all the other institutions still hanging onto the old paradigm, it didn't and still doesn't understand the millenial shift in human learning now underway.

Some Rays of Light

Some elements of the liberal church are moving in the direction of the new learning paradigm, however. Bob Parsonage, who heads an "Education in the Society" unit in the National Council of Churches, sees the systemic context of human learning. Verlyn Barker of the United Church of Christ has been working with Lawrence Cremin to formulate a learning system agenda for his denomination. Clyde Robinson has been doing much the same for the Presbyterian Church. Their thinking and advocacy are further along than anything coming out of K–12 and higher education. The leadership must now become involved in understanding these issues and in coalition building.

A Simple Agenda
for the Church

During a weekend workshop in Scranton during the spring of 1983 a simple, positive agenda for the church finally came into focus. Now that the expanded intentional life learning agenda has become clear, the church can become an active support and guidance agency for its members as they engage it.

This point is fundamental to the strengthening of the church's role in the new learning paradigm. Unless it learns its new role, it will continue to decline. The church and all institutions need to learn how to provide life planning and other kinds of guidance as we expand our agenda of explicit and intentional learning to replace the old indoctrinations. The church has the opportunity to be once again a key institution in value, role, and affective learning. It can also contribute to the strengthening of family and community life through participation in local learning coalitions.

The conservative and fundamentalist churches that have never left the indoctrinating mode and have provided their members with the basis for coherence and balance during these transitional decades will also be affected. As the new learning paradigm comes into being, and as institutions begin to make an impact, these churches will feel modernizing pressures they have not faced since the 1930s and '40s.

Let us now explore the role of the church in the implementation of the six strategies to accelerate the new learning paradigm.

Orienting the Citizen Learner

The church has been in the people orientation business for several thousand years and has had the best network of local institutions and people capable of such orientation. It now could play a vital role in orienting the public to the new American watershed and the learning tasks of its challenges. I say "could" because only a handful of church people seem to be aware of these challenges.

A turnabout could come quickly, however, as it did twenty years ago when the vision, courage, and leadership of the black church inspired a moral vision that swept the liberal church as a whole and brought it into the civil rights movement. Many of us remember vividly black and white clergy marching arm in arm on behalf of social justice and freedom and major denominations jumping in with support as the movement traveled north. My memories of a vibrant campus ministry helping students sharpen their understanding and support of the movement testify to that era's prophetic vision and action. Recently I find campus ministers nostalgic for those activist days but somehow uninterested in understanding the present watershed challenges.

But the present challenges are in many respects a continuation of the human and community development issues of that earlier era, with the added dimension of an economic transformation. Though the high drama of the civil rights movement's confrontations and riots are missing now, the stakes are higher. If the economic transformation proceeds without an improved sense of equity, the gains of the sixties will be lost in a growing and permanent underclass. If the economic transformation proceeds without a parallel re-creation of community and an enhanced personal development process, our nation's primary ethic could be even more firmly established as the financial "bottom line." I am somewhat optimistic about the rise in church consciousness from recent conversations with some senior staffers of the National Council of Churches, but, on the whole, the church, schools, and higher education are all looking inward at a time when we most need them to provide energetic moral leadership.

The church's loose organization permits innovation at local levels, so individual churches, campus ministers, and church-related colleges could become prototypes for engaging watershed issues and orienting people unilaterally or in concert with other institutions.

Linking the Institutions in the Learning System

Within some Protestant denominations the Hal Viehmans, Verlyn Barkers, and Clyde Robinsons are providing vision and leadership based on the fact that human learning occurs in many settings. In the Philadelphia-based CLEO project, Father Don McLean, president of St. Joseph's University, Brother Patrick Ellis, president of LaSalle College, and Sister Isabel Kneiss, president of Gwynedd Mercy College, have strongly supported the institutional linking strategy. The church managed earlier learning systems in coalition with family and other community institutions, so the strategy should be familiar.

Local churches have as good a chance as any institution to lead the coalition building, although politicians may do it first. Within every congregation are influential leaders in business, school, and civic affairs. A minister could begin the dialogue, as clergy sit on most important boards. Local church councils could orient themselves and stimulate the coalition building, once the understanding and commitment are in place.

Sharpening the Goal-Setting Process

The church has more opportunity for encouraging an enhanced and sharpened goal-setting process than any other institution.

On the level of individual members, the church could support the life planning process more openly than most other institutions. Shared religious beliefs and a familial ambience create a nurturing climate for exploring one's theory of living, assessing one's current condition, and resetting one's life goals.

Churches could develop the new family planning and goal-setting process discussed in Chapter Seven. As modern families grapple with ways to construct productive family lives, they need new supportive processes, and after a little research and development, churches would be in the best position for giving this support.

The church can strengthen the entire congregation's sense of community. It can broaden its agenda to examine the communal quality of life within the church and outside it. As congregations make their assessments and move on to set goals for improving communal life, they will lay the foundation for participating in the strengthening of the larger community, nation, and planet.

Developing Institutional Awareness and Adjustments

There are special problems in raising the institutional awareness of the church compared to the other institutions. Business had a clear signal that the economy needed transformation and has no alternative but to do it. After self-criticism, it developed new ideas and strategies and sparked a thrilling sense of engagement in its energetic young professionals. Education now hears the signal for change and soon must respond; community colleges are harbingers of what will ultimately come from the other educational segments.

We have no tradition in this country of criticizing the church as we do education. But if business sees its own faults and we all blame education for our ills, why can't we criticize the churches? After all, the church has a history of accommodating changing realities and new knowledge. We still behave as though the institutional church has revealed truth in all matters, and we are reluctant to challenge it except as adolescents. This puts the burden of criticism on the church itself.

Even worse than saying the church must do its own criticism, our failure to criticize says the church is no longer important. Of all the cultural commentary I've read in recent years, only Peter and Brigette Berger's book on the American family, *The War Over the Family*, sees the church's importance in shaping national character. Robert Nisbet's *History of the Idea of Progress* also mentions the probable importance of the church in the future, but only as part of a return to a darker age.

So let's screw up our courage and remind the church that it is an important institution in the life learning enterprise and needs to do better. Perhaps then we can help the Viehmans, Barkers, Robinsons, and all the others who have been trying to do the consciousness raising from the inside.

The adjustments are no different from those required in the schools, colleges, and other institutions in the learning system. First, the churches need to understand the expanded life learning tasks confronting individuals and the relationship of these tasks to the economic transformation and the re-creation of the community. Second, clergy and other church people need to develop the competencies and processes to support others in the assessment, goal setting, and implementation of life, family, and community plans. The church has as much of a chance as any other institution or profession of showing some inventive leadership, provided it acts soon.

Devising New Ways to Support
Expanded Intentional Learning

The church is in an excellent position to facilitate the trend to expanded intentional learning. The content of the expanded intentional learning agenda includes value and affective learnings that the church used to manage through its earlier indoctrination curriculum. The church's failure to adjust to the intentional learning mode has led us to put value clarification, sex education, and family life education into the school's portfolio, generating much conflict, given the pluralism of American society.

I look forward to the day when families and churches are more competent in these matters, take some of the heat off the schools, and through learning coalitions work cooperatively with all of the life learning institutions to ensure that the relevant life learnings are acquired.

Adjusting to High-Technology
Delivery Systems

There is much handwringing in church circles about the advent of the electronic and high-tech age. The church is well aware of radio and television's power and feels as impotent as concerned parents and educational groups about controlling it. The liberal church is also nervous about the growing electronic church, and the computer's influence on our lives makes everybody nervous.

But unless churches involve themselves in the systems and software development process, they will never gain a modicum of control. Church involvement, like that of education, requires new organizational inventions. No neighborhood church, school, or college is going to run a cable channel or make the heavy front-end investment required for software development. While some organizational inventions have led to satellite-based religious cable channels and undoubtedly will lead to others primarily concerned with religious programming, the concern here is with church involvement in the broader learning coalitions and in their implementation of the expanded life learning agenda.

Such broader learning coalitions could operate local cable channels oriented to the curricula of life learning rather than to the narrow K–12 or higher education programming based on the old learning paradigm. I proposed this on behalf of CLEO during the early cable franchising negotiations in Philadelphia in 1982, suggesting that a Philadelphia Learning Loop be created under the sponsorship of all the learning system institutions. It still is a possibility. The Delaware County learning system project led by the County Community College in association with other institutions including some churches is exploring an interconnection of the seven cable systems in the county as a life learning communications and support mechanism. Related inventions are possible around the country.

Computer software offers even more possibilities. Dick Bolles's *Three Boxes of Life* and *What Color Is Your Parachute?* could be replicated easily in computer software. Such programs could be oriented denominationally or ecumenically. Future Sunday Schools would have youngsters working on church-based personal computers or home loan software. The possibilities are endless once we leave the present paradigm and its obsolete delivery systems. The first generation of such software is beginning to appear. Jewish boys can now prepare for their Bar Mitzvah with the help of a computer program. A software package for Catholic schools to test religious knowledge, attitudes, and skills has just been made available. "Family Bible Fun" is a computer program aimed at Christian families. In "Game of the Maccabees" a Jewish-Syrian shootout that occurred in 165 B.C. can be reexperienced on the home computer. The adjustment has begun.

A Springboard for Renewal

The new American watershed and the rapidly emerging new learning system present the religious community with a big problem and a big opportunity. Business and education are beginning to adjust, but the church, with some exceptions, seems content to accept its decline. But it does have a once-in-a-century opportunity to reshape its role through support of the expanded intentional learning agenda, and especially those learnings that were once the province of the church. To do so it must return to the "people business" in a new and vital way. The present vacuum soon will be filled, and whether or not the church will rise to help fill it is one of the most interesting questions of this century.

CHAPTER 10

The Media: More Responsible Troubadours

The Original Troubadours

You may have found it interesting that the media are barely mentioned if at all in the national reports criticizing education. Having established that our younger generation spends more time watching television than in the classroom, you would think some reports would have explored the role and impact of media in the national learning process. Our failure to conceive of them as an important top- and bottom-of-the-iceberg learning institution and to hold them accountable for the learning they provide is a mystery.

Frank Mankiewicz, late of National Public Radio, concluded in *Remote Control* that television behaves as a kind of modern troubadour. In the Middle Ages troubadours brightened an otherwise boring existence by bringing new songs, gossip, and ideas to town, village, and castle. As they entertained they also stimulated our third human nature, our curiosity and readiness for change. If they offended they were sent on to the next town.

Mankiewicz worries about a society in which the troubadour becomes a mainstream institution, impacting the development of our people but not accountable for its effects. Many people share this concern, though they have never become a political force. Peggy Charren, head of Action for Children's Television, has been pushing an accountability agenda for children's programming for many years. Vance Packard also has questioned the instructional impact of television. But all the learning institutions from school to church have accepted the status quo as inevitable.

The Rise of an Institution

The rise of the media began in the last century with the arrival of the great newspapers and magazines. They enhanced the learning process of their time and gave our great-grandparents a richer sense of the world, their nation, their communities, and their own lives. The media helped start wars and affected politics, fashion, and behavior. When Horace Greely said, "Go west, young man," many young men listened.

When radio appeared in 1922, Herbert Hoover, then Secretary of Commerce, told the audience of the first Radio Conference of America that this medium would contribute to the development of the individual, strengthen family life, bring communities together, and even promote a sense of national identity and purpose; it would be a boon to human learning. Hoover then warned that commercial domination was the greatest threat to its usefulness. For a time colleges and universities used the radio to extend their educational and utilitarian mission, but with the cutbacks brought on by the Great Depression, educational radio retreated and never became a vital force.

Television arrived after World War II, both augmenting and replacing radio as the medium through which we received most of our entertainment and much of our information. Television and the daily paper, the vast array of magazines, the theater, and the movies—the American media became both big business and a big force in our lives. We've never been clear about their public purpose, however. The FCC Act of 1934 was built on the premise that the airwaves belong to the people and that the granting of a broadcast station franchise entailed some measure of public responsibility. This resulted in public affairs programming and the obligation to provide an opportunity for the expression of opposing points of view. But unlike many other countries where they are state controlled and operated, the electronic media here are relatively free to do whatever attracts listeners and viewers and whatever makes money. The profits versus public service issue has never been a loud one, and the Reagan administration has sought to deregulate both radio and television even further.

Media Indoctrinate As Well As Instruct Us

The issue of how effective an instructional instrument the media are in our larger sense of life learnings has never been settled either. For every research study proving that television violence leads to viewer violence, another fails to prove the connection. The industry is well aware that it is affecting listener and viewer behavior, attitudes, values, and choice;

advertisers wouldn't spend billions if it didn't. However, nothing like the continuing theoretical and research effort to understand the effects of the schools has yet been made with the media.

In 1978 I became a member of the Pennsylvania Public Television Network Commission (PPTN) and have since become chairman of its long-range planning effort. Good academic that I was, I tried to read everything in sight to be a competent commissioner. I began with Herbert Hoover and worked my way to the present. I was absolutely amazed with the thinness of most of the material.

No other major area of American life has such a shallow intellectual and research base. While there is a growing academic base in communications, it is too little and too late. Big thinkers are few and far between, and most of the coursework in colleges and universities is concerned with the nuts and bolts of newspaper, radio, television, and film production.

Given this paltry foundation, it is not surprising that we don't know much, even though most of us have many beliefs about the media's effect. The nightly news, documentaries, the "Nova," "National Geographic Special," Bronowski, Galbraith, and Sagan series, and untold other information- and concept-laden programs have enhanced our understanding of the world we live in. Don't we have a special relationship of trust with professor-mentors such as Walter Cronkite, Phil Donahue, and Alistair Cooke, as well as the many talk-radio hosts, psychologists, financial advisors, garden experts, etc., that now are making radio an intimate life learning medium?

In recent years I've begun to wake up in the middle of the night. My head turns on and keeps me awake. I've learned to switch on a talk show to turn off my head and help me drop back to sleep. I've become addicted to the "Larry King Show," which won a Peabody Award in 1983 and is as fascinating a learning experience as any I've ever had in academia. Larry runs a seminar with his listeners every night and doesn't mind that I go back to sleep when I'm ready!

The media clearly have met some of Herbert Hoover's aspirations. They allowed us to share major events like elections, the Kennedy assassination, the space program, and the Bicentennial, which bind us together in a common experience. They allowed us also to share danger as the Vietnam War, Watergate, the Tylenol story, and hurricanes and other natural disasters came into our homes.

While most of us believe that the media have bestowed profound benefits on us, don't we also believe they have some profound negative effects, such as the indoctrinations of soap opera and sit-com roles and values? The industry will retort with a troubadour's answer that it is just reflecting American life as it is. Parent, teacher, and preacher do not play to the lowest common denominator, however. The troubadour's answer is not good enough when we recognize that the media have as much power to indoctrinate as family, church, and community put together.

Can the Media Build Heroes, Create Visions?

My second concern is the media's bias toward criticism. Building images of leadership and heroism, with the possible exception of sports, is infinitely more difficult under this influence. Pennsylvania State Senator Richard Snyder, a Republican from Lancaster County and a valued colleague on the Pennsylvania Public Television Network Commission, is strong on this issue. In a spring 1983 speech to the Pennsylvania chapter of the American Association of University Professors, Snyder talked about the nation's need for heroes and wondered whether Abraham Lincoln's Gettysburg Address would have been accorded greatness today. He concocted a scenario in which Dan Rather introduced Lincoln by outlining all of his political and Civil War problems and indicating that he had come to Gettysburg to try to mend some fences and pull some chestnuts out of the fire. After the speech Rather would have summarized it, concluding that there really was nothing new said in Gettysburg.

Does the media have a responsible and accountable role in helping us build our visions, hopes, and heroes as we move through this watershed, or is its bias toward criticism, investigative reporting, and bad news, important as these activities are, the best we can expect? In *Without Fear or Favor*, Harrison Salisbury's memoir of the *New York Times*, Salisbury raises the same question. Writing in the wake of Watergate and a number of landmark court decisions enlarging the media's powers, he wonders whether the media can rise to the enhanced responsibilities that go with their new powers.

If all the institutions in the national learning system come to understand the challenges of the new American watershed and make the necessary adjustments and the media do not, I believe we'll still fall short of our goals. The media must become more responsible if we are to move quickly and smoothly through this transitional time.

A Blind Spot in the Critical Eye

As the challenge of economic transformation comes into focus, we can look back and credit the media with an excellent job of reporting the pieces of the crisis leading up to it. The nightly news super-star anchors and an array of follow-up documentaries kept us current on the realities and dangers of double-digit inflation and the failures of the Democrats to cope with it. This helped create the climate for Reagan's election. The media then turned their critical eye to supply-side economics, the human cost of the social programs' cutback, our loss of position in international competition, and the need for something other than business-as-usual in strengthening the economy. We all have a fairly good information and concept base about what needs to be done.

But as the economic lens has focused closer on human productivity, improved education, and the need for greater inventiveness, only the business publications have done a credible job of alerting us, and they speak to a constituency that is already knowledgeable and doing something about it. The rest of the media are content with having pinned the blame on the schools, and I see no evidence that the media have asked themselves what they could do to help us all "work smarter."

The Media's Invisible Curriculum

The invisible curriculum of the media continues as before, pushing us all to be self-fulfilling consumers, as their priority is the financial bottom line. Only the cutting-edge radio stations and the Larry King-type talk shows are stretching us to see some of the life learning adjustments. The deregulation tendencies continue as before, just as the great public challenges begin to come into focus.

Although the media help us share key national events and thus meet the Herbert Hoover goal of bringing us together as a nation, their role in neighborhood, community, region, and state identity building is essentially negative because of the overwhelming national focus. Even locally sponsored and supported public broadcasting stations heavily emphasize national news and programming.

Only talk-show hosts and newspaper columnist-advisors are engaging the challenge of personal and family development. Prime-time television still plays to the lowest common denominator in its soaps and sit-coms.

Some argue that it has never been the media's job to develop people, their communities, and the economy. But why not? We have seen that American higher education has had a reasonably successful century, even with an unfinished theory of its mission and tasks. The debate on the media's public purposes is also unfinished, and we have left the definition almost entirely to the media themselves. That's not the way a "good society" works. But the media have grown so big and powerful so quickly that they intimidate the other institutions that ought to care and be vigilant.

The watershed challenges will reopen the debate on public purpose, and it might make good corporate sense for the media to set up a "skunk works" to ask the presently unthinkable questions. If consumers, educators, politicians, and church people have given up on the big questions, business leadership may renew the debate out of self-interest. If creative, intelligent, hard working, and committed people are essential to the economic transformation, and if business's own advertising is not contributing to a renewed and contemporary work ethic, business leadership may well start pressing the media to help in meeting the challenges.

As the watershed challenges come to center stage, the media are trying to chart their futures in a very turbulent environment. Within the telecommunications field the breakup of the Bell system is reshaping personal and corporate communications. The growth of local cable systems challenges the networks to fight the newcomers with adjustments of their own. Roof-top antennas promise to challenge cable as each of us can pick up satellite signals (for pay, of course) directly. The entry of the home computer, the ease of accessing data bases around the world, and electronic mail are changing how we communicate. Many new players have entered the field, each trying to exploit the new hardware with new consumer services to grab their market share as quickly as possible. This great example of free enterprise is taking place in a pre-watershed mentality, however. The seriousness of the changes we're going through is generally unknown and unappreciated. There are new obligations as well as new markets, once the watershed challenges and the emergence of the new learning paradigm are understood.

A New Mission

As we think about the emerging public purposes of the media, let me turn to my favorite and one of the great national inventions, public broadcasting. The quality of its programming, almost all initiated at local levels, puts much of commercial broadcasting to shame. Public broadcasters could lead the way in raising public consciousness to the watershed challenges, but they haven't seriously explored what the "public" in their name might mean. After the creative burst that enlarged public broadcasting from its initial role of disseminating educational materials to schools, the thinking stopped. "Carnegie II," the most recent policy study, was an exercise in special pleading that offered no new visions and got nowhere. Even the fifty-four public television stations licensed to universities do little to extend their institution's resources and mission to their viewing regions.

With declining federal support and with National Public Radio's near financial disaster, public broadcasters have been in a survival mode, not much interested in a debate on public purposes. But the implications of the new American watershed and the emerging learning paradigm could give public broadcasting a competitive edge on its commercial colleagues in building new markets, new sources of support, *and* a new, distinctive public mission. One step in this direction was taken in June 1983 when the Philadelphia Public Television Network Commission adopted the recommendation of my long-range planning committee that the commission and the seven member Pennsylvania stations take the lead in bringing the implications and imperatives of the watershed challenges to twelve million Pennsylvanians.

One good example of how this might be done was seen in the November 1983 airing of "The Chemical People" by WQED-TV, our Pittsburgh station. This program on drug and alcohol abuse among young people was great in and of itself. It was shown after extensive preparations by a number of national, state, and local groups who arranged to have community groups or town meetings assembled to watch the program and then discuss what needed to be done at local levels. Just imagine how we could take that model as a base for personal, local, state, and national assessment, goal setting, and action on any shared personal or public issue. If we build on this energetic and creative effort of Lloyd Kaiser and his people at WQED, we might take a giant step toward engaging the watershed challenges using our extensive public broadcasting capability. Now let us further explore the media's role in moving along our six implementing strategies.

Orienting the Citizen Learner

We have the capability to receive bad news almost instantaneously. The Tylenol poisonings, the attempted assassination of the Pope, the downing of the Korean Air Lines 747, and thousands of similar stories reached us almost immediately. Some good news comes as quickly, such as the moon shot, space shuttle flights, a key victory in the Olympics, and other exciting events. The marketing of a new product, especially a new life-saving or pain-killing drug, reaches our collective or selective attention quickly when there's money behind it. But only "Sesame Street," "The Electric Company," and a handful of other programs have sought to provide the necessary orientation for lifelong learning. Newspaper columns tell what is wrong with the schools, but how to help kids, young people, and their parents with an orientation to life learning tasks is not considered news. Magazines such as *Woman's Day, Better Homes and Gardens,* and *Glamour* do a better job of orienting a nation of citizen learners than the rest of the media.

The indictment may seem unfair, since church, community, politicians, and families have not successfully oriented the citizen learner either. Something is wrong, however, when our primary means of getting information—which ought to be stimulating, thoughtful analysis—cannot move beyond the superficial and critical. I like to think Edward Murrow and Eric Severeid would have done better.

An example of how the media can speed up the dissemination of an idea can be seen in what the Temple Faculty Seminar did a few years ago. We put together a half-hour videotape on the higher education crisis and sold (at cost) about fifty copies to colleges and universities around the country. We didn't get the new paradigm over the top, but we saved travel expenses and repetitive speech making.

A documentary series on the new American watershed and the emerging learning paradigm would be an ideal vehicle for facilitating our adjustments. An even better approach would be a series of television documentaries with a coordinated series in local newspapers supported by relevant background reading available in the local library. A sitdown meeting sponsored by the local learning coalition would then synergize the separate efforts and result in shared understandings and action programs.

Best of all, if the American president were to lead off such a series and become the transforming leader the new American watershed requires, he would not only inform the nation about the new challenges and learning tasks we're facing, but would call on the learning system institutions to form local voluntary learning coalitions and begin the assessment, goal-setting, and implementation process.

Linking the Institutions in the Learning System

Given the state of our institutions, I'm inclined to look for leadership from the politicians once they embrace the new learning paradigm, but the media could lead as well. Editorials from local papers, radio, or television stations could give the initial call to convene the players. A series of feature articles could conclude with a similar call.

Bob Larson, president of WITF-TV, the Harrisburg, Pennsylvania public television station, several years ago pulled together the representatives of several public and private agencies to acquaint them with the new telecommunications environment and its implications. He proposed that they continue working together and invent new ways of doing business in such an environment. The emerging coalition, COM-NET, is just the sort of group that could be oriented to the watershed and begin to strengthen the Harrisburg learning system.

Even if the media do not take the lead in convening learning system institutions, they can be very useful in reporting subsequent progress, making editorial comment, and giving the public the necessary background information. For the re-creation of community agendas, the media are central to the distribution of the necessary community data base as a foundation for goal setting and helping the process become an annual community event.

Sharpening the Goal-Setting Process

The media have supported and accelerated the trend to more explicit goal setting. They have given us a sense of urgency about the economic transformation, the state of our communities, and the quality of our personal lives. In many instances the news and editorial messages have supported specific goal-setting processes and the resulting goals. On balance, we are doing better in goal setting than ever before, but given the scope of the watershed challenges we need to do better, and the media have a central role to play in this.

In 1982 Philadelphia celebrated its Tricentennial. As part of the celebration a comprehensive assessment and goal-setting process was organized by Ted Hershberg, the director of the University of Pennsylvania's Center for Philadelphia Studies. Hershberg put together several task forces to assess and recommend action on various aspects of community life. Faithful to the Naisbett participatory megatrend, they labored long and hard to produce a series of excellent reports. Both print and electronic media supported the project, giving it wide publicity at the outset, at the end, and with follow-ups. But a year later most of us who were close to the process concluded that it did not change much. Most of the recommendations were gathering dust. The goal-setting process needs to be linked tightly to implementation. But Philadelphia, like most cities, is deficient in such linkage. Had the political and civic leadership played their roles more effectively and exploited the project, its payoff would have been greater.

If the media understood the sharper goal-setting megatrend and wished to help accelerate its implementation in their communities, they would recognize the need for better connections between goal setting and implementation. Second, the media would recognize that discussion of public economic and communal goals needs to be continuous. The development of civic literacy and competence is a continuing undertaking, unlike a fleeting news story. Third, the media must help people understand how they can contribute to the process.

Concerning personal development, any media initiative in orienting the public to expanded life learning tasks can be tied together with guidance on the personal goal-setting process. Much of this occurs already in magazines, through talk-show psychologists, and feature writers, but it generally lacks the comprehensive life planning framework discussed earlier. Above all, the media need to see themselves as an integral part of the American learning system.

Developing Institutional Awareness and Adjustments

As the watershed challenges and new learning tasks have come into national consciousness, the media have been quick to join in developing the required institutional awareness and advocating the necessary adjustments within key institutions. They have helped sensitize businessmen and politicians to the scope of the economic challenges. As the human resource dimension became visible, they have joined in the criticism of American education. It is a start and illustrates the instructional effectiveness of the media as new issues and imperatives come into view, but it falls short. The real issue is whether the media are ready to understand and accept their responsibility for their role in the life learning process, especially television as the new indoctrinating agency in our lives.

Devising New Ways to Support Expanded Intentional Learning

The media, especially television, have helped fill the vacuum left by the decline of the traditional indoctrinating agencies by providing some bottom-of-the-iceberg learning, and they now have the opportunity to support our expanded intentional learning agenda. As each of us comes to a greater critical consciousness of what we need to learn and as we develop an enhanced commitment to the life learning process, we approach every life setting and experience ready to exploit it for its intentional learning potential. Just consider the level of consciousness that a contemporary woman brings to a reading of Ibsen's *A Doll's House* today compared to the level of feminist consciousness at the time of its publication. By helping us sharpen our understanding of the life learning process, the media could develop a generation of learners who will approach the troubadours' wares with a new critical consciousness, more resistant to indoctrination, more active in using those wares in the life learning process.

Suppose a television presentation of *A Doll's House* or any other fictional program is presented with an analytic and interpretive "wrap-around" which would enhance the viewer's intentionality and could increase the program's contribution to the life learning process. The best example is Alistair Cooke's commentary for "Masterpiece Theater." He gives the stories' historical or cultural contexts before and after each segment, exploiting the intentional learning potential of even second-rate fare. Such programming with mentorlike commentators relating to various segments of the audience is a great opportunity for expanding intentional learning. Disc jockeys have played such a role, for better or for worse, for decades now. Walter Cronkite developed close relationships with his listeners and viewers that go far beyond the explicit news-reading role.

As more of us understand the expansion of the intentional learning agenda, much innovation can take place. As critical viewing and listening rises, the old fare will lose its appeal and certainly will be seen and heard differently. It may just turn out to be good business for the media to begin to support expanded intentional learning in new and creative ways.

Adjusting to High-Technology Delivery Systems

Suggesting that the media need to adjust to high technology is carrying coals to Newcastle. The media obviously are further along than any other institution, whether it is newspaper reporters composing their stories on word processors or Ted Turner bouncing twenty-four hours of news off a satellite to cable systems across the country.

The media will lose what is now nearly a monopoly position on high-tech delivery systems as other players and institutions become involved. Large corporations already have their own communications systems that are easily adapted to support their employees' learning. In addition to residential services, some cable systems extend their service to small and mid-sized business and other institutions. As we all become more self-directed learners in the high-tech age, the media are in a prime position to offer learning services free of classroom, campus, and time constraints.

Between Hoover and Big Brother

Since the 1920s radio and television have come to play an increasingly pervasive and dominating role in our lives. While the other media have been diminished to a degree, their aggregate scope and impact are staggering. Herbert Hoover's wish that the electronic media remain free from commercial domination has not been realized, but Orwell's fear of "Big Brother" state control of communications is not a reality either.

There is little evidence that either the commercial or public broadcasters understand how central they are to the new learning paradigm, but market forces may hasten that understanding and push for a new accountability. Business leaders are beginning to understand that indoctrinating consumerism is not good enough in the new economy. Moreover, as we develop the critical consciousness instrumental to an expanded intentional learning agenda, it will simply be good business for the media to respond. At the same time, I still look to public broadcasting to become the exemplary institution in defining a public mission against which all others must compare themselves.

CHAPTER 11

The Corporation: New Agent of Social Change?

Business Dons a White Hat

Watershed periods thrust one or more institutions into leadership positions, and they pull the rest along. It should be clear by now that I see *some* American corporations leading us in meeting the new watershed challenges. My old liberal friends may feel betrayed by this judgement; after all, we have railed together against the excesses of corporate power, worker exploitation, the despoiling of the environment, the control of the political process, and so forth. How could the "bad guys" suddenly turn up wearing white hats?

Corporate power still runs to excess, and without the social legislation of the past century to restrain this tendency, the bottom-line ethic would prevail over other values. But this time that ethic has begun to converge with other human values. If we are smart we will drop any knee-jerk anti-business bias we may have and work at the convergence. If we do we'll go far in re-creating community and strengthening personal development while meeting the goals of the economic transformation.

I do not want to suggest that business leaders sat down and concluded, after due deliberation, that it was time for the American corporation to become the nation's agent for social change. They did it because, as Satchel Paige once suggested, "something could be gaining on you," the something being foreign competitors. If the leadership is effective, it is as Shakespeare observed in *Twelfth Night*, ". . . some have greatness thrust upon them." The American corporation is becoming innovative because it must to survive, and it is concentrating on the human dimension because human competence is more essential today than it was in the mass industrial age.

Previous periods of economic transformation altered leadership roles. The mass industrial transformation led to the Progressive movement, an increasingly interventionist government, and a growing social infrastructure. Fifty years ago, in response to the Great Depression, a new liberal coalition including organized labor updated the social agenda. The labor movement even carried the banner for other humanizing initiatives beyond its immediate self-interests. Twenty years ago the fear of automation was a precipitating factor in the organization of the civil rights movement. When we moved instead into an era of great economic prosperity, the social initiatives of the Great Society, the counterculture represented in Reich's *The Greening of America*, and the human rights agenda all became possible.

The Macro Issues of Economic Transformation and the New Learning Paradigm

The proximate demands of the economic transformation are difficult enough, but we should look beyond to the larger context of the watershed challenges and their relevance to economic issues. This perspective may be easier to maintain now than at another time. After all, as business leaders work to strengthen their corporate culture as an explicit, intentional undertaking, it takes a very small step to see the need for strengthening the larger culture explicitly and intentionally. That's why business executives understand the new learning paradigm more quickly than any other group. The strengthening of corporate culture is tantamount to strengthening the company's learning system. If it can be done on the inside, why not in the rest of society?

Given this perspective, the tasks of economic transformation barely have begun. Despite my enthusiasm for corporate innovation, this characterizes only a handful of companies. Their success has not gone unnoticed by other companies, but the diffusion of the new management philosophy and process is just beginning.

While some of us deal with the macro issue of creating a new paradigm and others debate natural industrial policy, most businesses will follow the maxim of the excellent companies and "stick to the knitting" of running and strengthening their companies. They will be moving through a major learning experience as they shift from top-down and hierarchical management to more interactive and participatory modes. Most of this is bottom-of-the-iceberg learning, as everyone from the chief executive officer to the floor sweeper casts off old indoctrinated patterns and acquires new intentional learning. It's likely it will be more difficult for the sweeper to give up the old adversarial habits than for the CEO to stop being boss.

How Can We Increase Productivity?

If increased competitiveness and productivity are our continuing goals, and if workers' increased participation and commitment are instrumental to those goals, how are these qualities strengthened? In 1983 the White House Conference on Productivity spotlighted some management practices which seem to do just that by dealing with key issues. The first issue concerns employment security. Will the company keep me in hard times? Another issue concerns the we-they gap between management and other employees. Will top management share company information openly with all employees, even confidential information that might be leaked to competitors? Another asks: Are the reward systems "tailored to be sensitive to the nuances of performance?" Also, when the company does well, do all its members share in the gains as in the "gainsharing" plans now being tested around the country? Is the corporate culture structured so that anyone feels free to criticize or propose a wild idea? Does the climate stimulate rather than suppress inventiveness?

HRD People Are the Architects of Corporate Culture

A new breed of human resource development (HRD) manager is providing the in-house leadership for the corporate culture part of the economic transformation. Coming out of personnel or training backgrounds, these managers and their professional association, the American Society for Training and Development (ASTD), are the catalysts for the economic transformation. For many years they have had the same back-of-the-bus role in corporations that continuing educators have in higher education. Like them, human resource development people have suffered indignities and learned to survive by their wits, but they have stayed faithful to the vision that human capital is a company's fundamental asset. Now their time has come.

Unlike other educators, they know how to link their efforts to explicit and specific goals. They understand bottom-of-the-iceberg learning better than their counterparts elsewhere in the educational domain, and now they are the innovators in transforming organizations and remaking corporate cultures. Their capacity for self-criticism seems to keep them evolving. Having used T-groups to get at the affective and interpersonal reality of the workplace, they are now pushing for change in the organizational environment. Just as educators need to move beyond the classroom and school to the larger reaches of the learning system, these managers are leaving the training division to see the entire corporate culture as the proper site for human learning.

There is unevenness of investment in human resource development. Most large corporations invest heavily, but some make a minimal effort, preferring to hire away people who have been trained by someone else. Most small and mid-sized companies use consultants or just underinvest in this function.

The ASTD and other national organizations have sounded the bugle for greater investment in the development of human capital and are beginning to be heard. Proposals are being discussed ranging from tax incentives like those now available for capital improvements and research and development investment to payroll levies to fund Individual Training Accounts, which are much like Individual Retirement Accounts. Delaware's Secretary of Labor Dennis Carey has been promoting the use of the unemployment insurance system as a vehicle for a more equitable training and retraining system.

Education and the HRD Revolution

While the nation's colleges and universities are not leading the human resource development revolution, the door is open to them, especially through continuing education. Small and mid-sized companies will not reach parity with the larger corporations unless a new HRD support service is organized on their behalf. Through our work at CLEO we have sought to bring the resources of the Philadelphia higher education community to meet the needs of small and mid-sized business, and this has led to one of our more interesting inventions.

A year ago my friend and partner in paradigm shifting Judith Stoyle and I were wondering what we could do to plant the new learning paradigm at one of the many industrial parks and office centers springing up around the country. These often house 100 to 300 companies with 5,000 to 15,000 employees all working in the same contiguous space. Mostly small companies or remote divisions of larger companies, they generally don't have the capacity for a full-scale HRD program because each company behaves independently of the others. We began to think about an on-site, comprehensive set of HRD services which would be available to each company according to its own requirements. If we built that set of services on the megatrends and strategies of the new learning paradigm, we would not only be giving a leg up to any participating company and its individual employees, but would also be shaping an aggregate overall culture promoting enhanced human productivity among all its residents. To move toward such a goal we'd have to overcome the isolation of each company from the others and bring the higher education community closer to them. Working through CLEO as the regional higher education broker seemed to be the solution.

The EMO

We took the raw idea to Ed Mazze, dean of Temple's business school, who had enthusiastically supported our effort to bring the new learning paradigm to Temple. He is a natural-born marketer, and he liked the idea but suggested better packaging. After some reflection he suggested that we call the enterprise an EMO, building on the concept of the Health Maintenance Organization, or HMO. This is the system invented to move health care from an illness to a prevention orientation and to link it to the fringe benefit system of health insurance. Why not implement the new learning paradigm through a parallel device?

CLEO quickly adopted the idea and pursued a grant from the Fund for the Improvement of Post-Secondary Education to test out the idea in several different settings. Meanwhile, a new corporate center was being built nearby. Lois Lamdin, our CLEO executive, was exploring higher education's role in the center, and we began to see the Great Valley Corporate Center as the site for the first EMO.

The Great Valley Corporate Center

Until recently industrial parks and office centers have been run as real estate operations providing good transportation access and worksites remote from the rigors of urban life. But Bill Rouse, the driving force behind the Great Valley Corporate Center, had a different vision. Beyond its lovely setting in Chester County's rolling hills, Rouse wanted to create an environment and provide a set of services to his tenants that enhanced the quality of worklife, met a variety of shared individual and corporate needs, and contributed to the aggregate productivity of the entire community. Not an average landlord, Rouse already has built in a fitness center, supported the spontaneous creation of a softball league among the companies, set up a child care center, and is collaborating with CLEO in implementing the first EMO through a broad-spectrum Business Development Center.

Rouse's first step in helping bring the EMO to life was to organize a planning group of top managers from the resident companies. We shared our views on the obsolescence of the present learning paradigm and outlined the megatrends leading to the new paradigm. We then discussed the six implementing strategies as they might apply to all who work at the Center, to the individual companies, and to the Center as a whole. Those managers with extensive HRD experience quickly saw the value of the approach and agreed to initiating a goal-setting process between CLEO and the resident companies.

Concurrently we agreed that CLEO should offer a variety of services on-site as soon as possible. Rouse gave us a renovated farm house adjacent to the Center's restaurant to serve as an accessible headquarters. The learner services include information on all the programs of our member colleges, computer-based career and life guidance, assessment of prior learning to convert into college credit, customized training, a consultant bank, several college courses to be delivered on-site, life planning workshops, and conference planning and management services. Rouse is building a hotel-conference complex within the Center, and the EMO will eventually be headquartered there.

CLEO member colleges represent an array of resources, so we organized a twice-weekly lunch hour series of events ranging from lectures on business and other topics to string quartets, playlets, and art exhibits. In this way each CLEO member could soft sell its other wares. We also offered a business-oriented current books discussion group.

The strategic goal was to help every company sharpen its human resource goal setting to increase productivity and competitiveness and to help the people in the Center sharpen their personal goal setting through explicit life plans. Our next step is to identify the role the Center and its companies can play in strengthening the learning systems of the adjacent communities where many of their employees live.

As a pilot effort the first-stage financing is somewhat jerry-built with a lot of help from Rouse. The resident companies have to work out an assessment and financing procedure until we find a better way.

The linkage between the corporate and the higher education community through an EMO brings down the walls of each domain and stimulates a mutual planning and implementation process. An EMO can also be developed within a single company, among a consortium of small and mid-sized companies not contiguously located, or even at the community scale. The fundamental issue is that the EMO not become another brokering operation for the current old paradigm programs but that it become the vehicle for the new consciousness of the new learning paradigm. We hope to demonstrate its usefulness in several new settings.

Business Will Be the Major Influence in Strengthening Our Learning System

Upgrading the present labor force for the new economy will be taxing enough, but the business community must lead the strengthening of the pre-work learning system as well. Just as any business sets specifications for materials and services from suppliers and contractors, so will our public and private sector institutions that consume manpower communicate their needs to the colleges and schools that provide the manpower. In the vocational education and community college sectors, such linkage has had a long tradition, but the extent of the economic transformation is such that the scope and quality of such linkage needs a fundamental strengthening and review. New business/school and business/higher education committees, task forces, and councils appearing around the country are a very positive sign that the linkage problem is being engaged. But useful as it is for both sides to renew the long atrophied dialogue, my sense is that the dialogue is taking place within the old learning paradigm. Since the business community is closer to the new learning paradigm than the K–12 or higher education community, business has a special opportunity and responsibility to enlarge the vision of the educators.

As both sides consider the many skills, attitudes, and experiences instrumental to economic, societal, and personal goals, they can move past the present narrow, explicit curriculum and consider incorporating bottom-of-the-iceberg learning. This will move the dialogue very quickly past the school to other learning system institutions and to the system itself and will lay a foundation for the broader based learning coalitions. Economic goals threaten to dominate every dialogue, however, so it is up to the educators to advocate life learning to achieve not just economic goals but all the goals of the "good society."

Nevertheless, given its existing power and now its new vitality, American business probably will be the most influential institution in the strengthening of the American learning system during the next decade and beyond. We can only hope that business will use that influence in the implementation of the following six key strategies.

Orienting the Citizen Learner

Business can speed the public's orientation to the new learning tasks required by the watershed issues in three ways.

It can follow the example of ASTD and other educational associations trying to raise their member's awareness around the nation. The excellent companies are showing the way by shaping an expanded learning agenda for their employees. By using the company communications system and developing a new community-wide communications system at Rouse's Great Valley Corporate Center, CLEO is trying to orient all who work there to the new learning tasks. A New York Stock Exchange study showed that the example of the excellent companies was stimulating many others to rethink their philosophies and practices, and a few key prototypes of company-based learner orientation programs can foster others.

Second, the business community can work with other learning system institutions at local, state, and national levels. This is Dick DeCosmo's first priority at the Delaware County Community College— developing a partnership with local corporations and other learning system institutions and launching county-wide learner orientation processes. This is the kind of activity ASTD and a number of educational associations want to stimulate around the country.

Third, and perhaps most important, business must initiate a shift in its embedded messages in its advertising in print and electronic media. Through its shortsighted, and perhaps inadvertent, support of hedonistic consumerism, business has truly contributed to its own problem. By helping the media see their role and responsibility in raising standards and helping people understand the watershed challenges and new learning tasks that follow, it can speed the reorientation process.

Linking the Institutions in the Learning System

When I asked Bob Craig, vice-president of ASTD, what message I should underline in this book, he emphasized that ongoing communications and linkage among all institutions concerned with human learning were urgent and fundamental. ASTD has 50,000 members who are now being sensitized to show leadership in developing such linkage. Although chief executive officers will likely be the leaders in starting local learning coalitions, their HRD people will inject substance into the discussion. Therefore I urge all CEOs to make sure their HRD people's job descriptions include this external orientation.

As I have stressed repeatedly, the initial task of establishing linkage is bringing people together, and any institution in the learning system can do this: politicians, religious leaders, the media, or even educators. But because business has the most immediate stake in strengthening human learning and possibly now has more relevant expertise than other institutions, it can play to its own self-interest as well as that of the broader community by convening the parties, orienting them to the watershed challenges, and establishing common action agendas.

Sharpening the Goal-Setting Process

In spite of all the current contention about a national industrial policy, business and government are closely involved at municipal, county, regional, and state levels in economic goal setting and establishing follow-through mechanisms via tax incentives, customized job training supports, and a variety of other economic development inducements. But current goal-setting activities all are constrained by the old learning paradigm. They need to be enlarged within the concept of the new learning paradigm to stimulate inventiveness, entrepreneurship, risk taking, and group effectiveness. Most of the mechanisms are in place; only the concepts and strategies of the new paradigm need to be added.

By understanding that a re-created community and strengthened personal development are instrumental to economic performance, the American corporation can become a broad-spectrum societal change agent. The corporation is closer to that role at the moment than any other institution. I am not sanguine that it will fulfill that role. Therefore the rest of us need to renew our understanding of what needs to be done and show some leadership.

Developing Institutional Awareness and Adjustments

Economic transformation is rippling through the corporate world and bringing about awareness and adjustments, as the New York Stock Exchange study suggested. But the process has just begun, and business institutions must be kept on this track as we develop the supportive infrastructures.

Business has recognized how important the nation's human resources are to the economic transformation, but the old paradigm still dominates the adjustments. The megatrends of the new learning paradigm are on their way, and the faster we develop them, the faster we can strengthen the human resources. New paradigm adjustments can be made quickly within the corporate environment. Sharper goal setting identifies the human competencies and characteristics that will meet the goals, and explicit employee orientation and life planning service can lay the foundation for developing these traits, provided that a balance is maintained between company goals and employee life goals.

Only the large corporations have the staff capacity to do this, and we urgently need a supportive infrastructure for small and mid-sized companies. ASTD's consultant corps is one resource, but most of these people are not yet up to speed on the new learning paradigm. The higher education community is also a potential resource, but only after orientation to the new paradigm. Meanwhile, the small and mid-sized companies are at a disadvantage.

Devising New Ways to Support Expanded Intentional Learning

Paolo Frere, one of the most inventive educators of the century, was exiled from Brazil for trying to create a critical self-consciousness among the peasants so that they had a better sense of what they needed to learn and why. His goal was enhanced human dignity and economic well-being. Unhappily these goals were not instrumental to the proximate goals of the larger society at the time. Now we have the best companies creating that same critical self-consciousness to achieve company goals, resulting in a better understanding of what needs to be learned and why in order to strengthen corporate culture.

Anyone familiar with Sloan Wilson's poke at the fifties corporate culture in *The Man in the Gray Flannel Suit* might find a parallel in today's "dressing for success" trend. The difference, however, is that Wilson's gray people were the products of that era's embedded indoctrinating mechanisms, and today's young executives dress more intentionally, slightly amused by the uniform they wear. Young professional women wearing jogging shoes on the way to work make a statement about the importance of their uniform, the equivalent of the standard suit and necktie.

But the trend to an expanded intentional learning agenda based on heightened, critical self-consciousness is still in a very early stage of development. At the 1983 White House Conference on Productivity, C. Jackson Grayson appealed eloquently for an enlarged investment in human resource research and development. Much of this will nurture those human qualities instrumental to the economic transformation. The identification, care, and feeding of innovative "stars" in the workplace already is an explicit management strategy to support inventiveness, but who can tell where this will lead? The shift in understanding and attitudes toward these bottom-of-the-iceberg characteristics is revolutionary. Throughout human history the need to keep a tight rein on deviance has made most human cultures, corporate or otherwise, hostile to creativity, invention, and innovation. The creative person has struggled uphill for millenia. Just imagine the possibilities if it were otherwise.

As the corporate world learns how to nurture inventiveness within the company, it might also stimulate the nurturance of such qualities in the other institutions. Business might help the others make the necessary adjustments to expand their cultivation of inventiveness and the other new intentional learnings.

Adjusting to High-Technology Delivery Systems

The business community inevitably is further along in adapting internal communications and HRD systems to its own high-technology inventions. It can be truly helpful to other institutions in updating the way they deliver services. Schools, colleges, government agencies, nonprofit organizations, health care systems, and so forth all need help in adapting to the high-tech age. Generally business provides service through marketing, but selling a new piece of hardware or software without helping the buyer rethink the larger system adjustments creates as many problems as benefits. The introduction of micro computers into the nation's schools is a good example. Had computer manufacturers put more effort into working out the delivery system adjustments in cooperation with educators before the hard sell, the benefits would have outweighed the problems created.

One example of the creative application of the new technologies took place during the preparations for the 1983 White House Conference on Productivity. C. Jackson Grayson, former Nixon economic advisor and currently Chairman of the American Productivity Center, had been asked to develop some private sector recommendations for the Conference. Instead of commissioning a set of papers or conducting a number of fly-in, fly-out conferences, Grayson organized seven computer conferences on different aspects of the productivity problem, each with about twenty knowledgeable people and a moderator. After a fast day and a half at the Center in Houston to become computer conference competent and to organize a work program, we went home and proceeded to "conference" for the next four months.

It was by all means the best conference I ever attended. The participants could address the entire conference, sidebar with one or two others, and prepare a report and then vote on it—all via computer. The format promoted a sense of equality as all of us, even the famous, were a first name and a number. Even Garrison Keiller's "shy persons" had a better chance to participate than at a sit-down conference where the more assertive tend to dominate. Moreover we could "attend" the conference whenever it was convenient. (I typically signed on at 5:30 A.M.) Since we had time to think before we prepared our comments, the result was a more thoughtful conference as well. The only thing I missed was the eye-rolling, and that I could imagine.

The experience was so rewarding that Grayson organized a dozen continuing computer conferences on productivity involving busy executives and others who just could not participate in such activities any other way.

Over the Long Haul

I started this chapter with the radical judgement that the American corporation is the major societal change agent in the present watershed, and I will end with that characterization. The cutting-edge corporations are closer to understanding and implementing the new learning paradigm than any other institution. Because the corporation's basic mission is to make money, not necessarily a "good society," this development entails a new and heavy responsibility to use its leadership wisely. As the corporation moves past the myopic emphasis on the quarterly bottom line and the "paper entrepreneurship" that Robert Reich so aptly criticized to a more long-range interest in economic growth, it must also be mindful of the parallel challenges of personal and community development.

Just as the Progressive movement evolved a century ago to counter the excesses of the mass industrial transformation and to shape a renewed vision of the "good society" for most of this century, so today it is up to the public sector and nonprofit institutions to see that the economic transformation proceeds in the context of restated human and communal values. Walter Lippmann saw the problem coming many years ago and argued that the American university was the most likely institution to give us perspective and long-range guidance. Since neither the university nor any other public or nonprofit institution has stepped into that role as yet, the corporation may yet take that leadership position. This raises a deeper and more fundamental issue about the way we organize American society, an issue we need to prepare to debate.

CHAPTER 12

The Human Services Agenda

Change Is Hard for Newcomers

One advantage older institutions and professions have over recent arrivals is their history of change and adaptation. Politicians, educators, business leaders, and church people know their institutions have evolved, often under outside pressure. For newcomers the adaptation may come a little harder. I conclude this series of visits to the mainstream institutions by commenting on the application of the new learning paradigm for the human services, the setting of my first career.

The human services had a smashing youth as a creation of American Progressivism and the new psychology, then a productive middle age as the nation built a vast array of safety nets for the poor, handicapped, old, unemployed, and other populations at risk. But they have now fallen on hard times. The most visible sign is their lack of funds; however, the problem goes deeper. Just as educators need to adapt to a new learning paradigm, so do the human services, and the seeds of their renewal are in their very beginnings.

As I suggested earlier, the human services carried the new psychology to us in the early years of the century. The robust optimism that people could change with a little couch time, a little psychotherapy, a little casework, or a little counseling contributed magnificently to our present idea of human nature. They were the agent of a whole new set of freedoms and choices as the old beliefs and indoctrinations began to ebb around the turn of the century. There were the settlement houses helping new immigrants and the urban poor. There was that special concern for child welfare, providing free milk and maternal health care fifty years before such services became a public responsibility. Foster child and adoption practices were cleaned up and new standards established. Born of the idiosyncratic American left, human services workers joined with labor and other liberal forces in coalitions which later led to public housing, social security, welfare, unemployment compensation, collective bargaining, and other social legislation of the 1930s.

We Move into the Age of the Therapies

During the twenties as the seeds of psychoanalytic thought took root in the United States, the fledgling mental health movement grew over the next few decades into a variety of new therapies and the new professions of dynamic psychiatry, social casework, and clinical psychology. It led to a new stage of critical consciousness among the intelligencia and literati, reflected in thousands of *New Yorker* cartoons. After one had a sense of one's unconscious and the picturesque mental apparatus of Id, Ego, and Super-ego, slips of the tongue were no longer mistakes, and dreams were not a product of overeating. Every thought had more than one level of meaning.

There were excesses, of course, leading to my Niebuhrian law of anti-parsimony: Never make anything simple if you can possibly make it complex! During a visit to a psychoanalyst who had just undergone an emergency appendectomy, a colleague and I found our bedridden friend deep in thought. When we inquired why, he said he was trying to unravel the psychodynamics of his acute appendicitis. My colleague suggested that some days a banana was just a banana!

Evidence for the effectiveness of different therapies remains inconclusive, but the Age of the Therapies was a useful and necessary transition to a more explicit intentional approach to bottom-of-the-iceberg learning. Protected within the medical field, these agents of the new psychology avoided collision with the church and other tradition-protecting forces and laid the foundation in concept, practice, and legitimacy for the emerging learning paradigm.

I spent the 1950s as a clinical psychologist in several settings where the "mental health team" concept was practiced. Teams of psychiatrist, social worker, and clinical psychologist attended to a patient's every need. In theory the psychiatrist brought medical expertise, the psychologist measurement and testing skills, and the social worker the skills of working with families and other community agencies. There were pecking-order problems, with the MD psychiatrist feeling superior to the other two and the PhD psychologist feeling superior to the social worker who only had a master's degree. The latter two were able to share their common resentment toward the excessive authority and power of the psychiatrist. It's a wonder we did as well as we did.

Being a nonphysician on the faculties of two medical schools helped me understand the condition of lepers, blacks, and other undervalued people. Once I received extravagant praise from my MD supervisor for some good and creative work; the pat on the back was accompanied by the suggestion that I really ought to go to medical school!

I began to feel that the elevated level of professional authority, a hand-me-down from the ancient priests and witch doctors, was counterproductive in a democratic and increasingly egalitarian age. The issue finally surfaced during the turbulant sixties when para-professions were invented to aid client communications. The professions had grown too remote.

The Great Society Challenged the Professions

The 1950s were the high point for the human service professions. So many new psychologists were being produced that one statistician projected that there would be more psychologists than people by the year 2000! It was also the high point of professional status and authority. People were afraid to make parental, marital, or other life judgements without consulting a professional. The professions proliferated, reinforced by licensure and certification, and jobs abounded as more and more public funds went into mental health, welfare, counseling, and rehabilitation programs.

The social policy and legislation of the 1960s challenged the human services. The goals of the War on Poverty and a score of related manpower, education, health, and community development programs were to equalize opportunity by strengthening human development at the community level. For the first time the nation invested in an explicit and intentional human learning/development strategy that was totally at variance with the established therapeutic professions. All of the new programs, from Head Start, Job Corps, and Community Action to Model Cities and the cutting-edge community health and mental health programs, were staffed by the mavericks and the discontented from a variety of professions. As one of the latter I suspect we were like the first generation of Freudians, strange but interesting people who had come from a dozen other fields.

My deviance in signing on with the Great Society had a kind of rationality to it. I had become impatient with the therapies and had begun to work at community mental health strategies such as redoing Philadelphia's Skid Row and converting a prison into a rehabilitation center. The old social gospel urges from my Mennonite heritage were asserting themselves, and I moved to the frontiers of the Great Society.

The Great Society was flawed in many ways, including a very thin intellectual base. Money came so quickly that we never had time to think through the programs or train people to implement them. So most recruits did what they had done previously. The human development goals of enhanced competence and responsibility were distorted into the entitlement ethic. Martin Luther King, Jr.'s incremental change strategy was replaced by the impossible utopianism of the Black Power advocates. The lid slammed down, and the Great Society warriors retreated in disarray.

Because of the social turbulance of the sixties, the underlying premise that the nation's human learning and development process was no longer adequate never reached our consciousness. As the era ended, the learning system's defects remained unattended and quietly continued to grow until they became evident in today's watershed challenges. The human services went back to business as usual, and, once so sensitive to people's needs, they now focused on the needs of the professions.

Once Brash, Now Dull and Stuffy

The legitimacy crisis in American education has its counterpart in the human services. The Reagan cutbacks in social programs met no effective protests. The old fire was gone. It was obviously a time to regroup—to rethink and return to the fray with a new game plan. But the response has been remarkably like education's: Wait for the good old days to return so that we can go back to business as usual.

Instead, the first thing the human services must do is understand the watershed challenges, especially the need for fundamental economic transformation. The nation has neither the wealth nor the inclination now to fund the human service programs. The roles have reversed; the human services now are dull and stuffy while business is becoming brash and creative.

The challenges of re-creating community and strengthening personal development are humbling also. The growth of human services has not accelerated the decline of community and personal togetherness, though a statistician could make such a correlation, but they do no more than scratch at the edges of the problems we face. The human services were the product of the new psychology's message of freedom and choice, but in their eventual fixation on the therapies, they failed to provide the necessary life guidance for most people.

I've applied this criticism to all institutions, and the human services must not be defensive and play the victim. Defensiveness leads to rigidity, stultifies creativity, and prevents making the necessary adjustments in this transitional time.

Once the human services understand the changes they have negotiated in the past, they can develop a better sense of the emerging needs and adjust accordingly. There are continuing needs for the therapies. Many people are still subject to the convoluted learning to which we give diagnostic labels and they need special therapeutic attention, assuming, of course, that we will continue to advance the therapies past the early magical phase. Moreover, the services for children needing protection, the handicapped, the developmentally disabled, and all of the other groups at risk are still necessary.

The watershed issues and the emergence of a new learning paradigm offer a new set of opportunities to the human services for serving the American public. The family needs strengthening as an instructional unit and the community as an instructional environment. With their history of advocacy for the underdog, the human services also could serve as an ideological monitor to preserve as much equity as possible during this rapid transition.

Resources at Hand

Because there will be no new money for staff and organizations to take these assignments, the human services will have to use available resources more effectively. Just as I envision college professors enhancing their productivity by understanding and supporting students' broader life learning tasks without diminishing the scope or quality of their course-work, so I envision human service workers understanding and supporting the broader life learning tasks of their clients while continuing their current services.

For example, the Girl Scouts are moving into more intentional career and life planning, and family planning agencies could expand into more intentional family life development activities in addition to their current functions. Hospital and physician waiting rooms could carry an entirely new set of messages and materials to reinforce the trend to expanded intentional learning and sharper goal setting.

First, institutional and professional consciousness must be raised through learning coalitions such as those described in previous chapters. Human service agencies and organizations can contribute to the strengthening of community and make their ideological pitch for equity for all citizens. As we raise standards and reward quality performance, we will be tempted to denigrate the losers. The human services need to balance the drive for excellence with a maintenance of a common humanity for all, building on their heritage of advocacy for the underdog.

Most of all, they can help strengthen underclass communities, which have urgently needed attention ever since the human service professionals retreated during the turbulence of the sixties. The urban politics of the eighties still make it difficult for "outsiders" to help out, and, indeed, few citizens are interested in helping. But as we mobilize our communities to engage the watershed challenges, the underclass, the functionally illiterate, should not be singled out; we all have new learning tasks to perform. The human services may have a special role to play in fortifying underclass communities within this collective effort.

After a heady youth and vigorous middle age, the human services seem to face a grim future. This condition is no different from that of any other institution, however. The human services, like the other institutions, need to restore their moral vision and then contribute to building a broader vision of the "good society" and the "good life." After a busy century of building new professions and institutions with which to implement the founding vision, it seems that vision has been dimmed by the trappings of professionalism and bureaucracy. It needs to be sharpened and illuminated again. It wasn't a bad vision and might be useful for another century.

CHAPTER 13

A Note on International Applications

Learning Crises Are Developing in Europe Too

A few years ago I discussed the emerging learning paradigm with Dick Smethurst, who is responsible for continuing education at Oxford University in England. Smethurst was intrigued with the ideas, especially with the notion that the old indoctrinations can drop out of the learning system without anyone being aware that this is happening or doing anything to replace the lost learning in a more intentional mode. He observed that the English learning system seemed to be a decade or two behind ours and that perhaps it was time to think about applying the model there as well.

As I read about other Western European societies and especially the malaise of their youth, I suspect that watershed challenges are developing there too. Modernizing trends are worldwide, and it is inevitable that the old indoctrinations are being lost elsewhere, though to varying degrees and at different rates. Unless a society becomes more sensitive to the subtle shifts in its learning system, especially those at the bottom of the iceberg, problems could develop and fester with no observable symptoms until they become a full-blown crisis.

A Lesson from Adolescence

I presume no expertise in international affairs, but a compelling personal experience in India in 1966 suggests possible international applications of the human learning system model. My strategic goal back then was to deepen the American university's contribution to the urban community development process. One of my Indian colleagues came to believe that Indian universities might contribute more to their country's development if they adopted some of the policies and strategies we were implementing during that decade's urban crisis. Before I knew it we had an invitation from the Indian Secretary of Education and sponsorship from the United States Information Agency of the U.S. Department of State.

We assembled a team from Brandeis University and the Universities of Minnesota, Wisconsin, and California to spend a month making the rounds of Indian universities and holding three major conferences (in Calcutta, New Delhi, and Jaipur) with our Indian counterparts. It was a fascinating and disquieting experience. In addition to the usual miseries afflicting that country student disturbances had shut down a third of the universities when we arrived. Adults told us all sorts of stories about the new generation's criminal tendencies and why the perpetrators should be thrown in jail.

As I visited and spoke at the universities that were open, I spent some time with students alone and informally. I found them to be bright, well-mannered, and totally engaging young people, and we had some marvelous conversations. As I probed for the source of the strikes and unrest, I found that the complaints were against the adults' insensitivity to student needs and rights. After hearing this at several different universities, I concluded that adolescence had come to India, but that the adults were still blind to its implications for the management of young people.

Americans have come to expect a certain level of independence, striving, and rebellion against established authority during the adolescent years, and we've learned to roll with the punches. We may even be concerned when these behaviors don't arrive on time. But there seemed to be no precedent for such understanding, anticipation, or accommodation within the Indian universities then. If I was right, any American dean of students would have poured some oil on the troubled waters and adjusted the institution's authority structure and process, as we have done throughout the century. Even though the American professoriate and the formal curricula do not acknowledge bottom-of-the-iceberg learning, deans of students are well aware of them and cope with them daily.

Indian youth were losing their old respect/fear/acceptance of authority and were asserting a new set of "rights." I wouldn't have used the term "learning system" at the time, but the Indian system was changing in ways that the educators didn't understand and to which they did not adjust. I trust they have done better since, but even the U.S. student movement caught many of us by surprise.

During a ceremonial tea with the governor of the State of Rajastan toward the end of our visits, my friend and colleague Sandy Kravitz, then representing Brandeis University, began to remonstrate with the governor about misunderstandings between the students and the generation in power. Kravitz asked boldly, "Why don't you give some power to the students?" After a moment's hesitation, and with a sly look, the governor answered, "You cannot give power; it must be taken." I have never forgotten the wisdom of that remark!

By the end of our trip we had made considerable progress toward our goal of organizing a bilateral project between the American and Indian universities to collaborate on the urban community development agenda. We were lining up funding from several government agencies and private foundations when it was revealed that one of the foundations was a CIA front. That ended the project and friendly Indo-U.S. relations for a while. We took the next plane home.

Can an Educational Model Be Exported?

The United States and Europe have been exporting educational models to the third world ever since the colonial era. My experience in India made me wonder whether we were not also sending out embedded assumptions geared to our own societies and to the time at which the model was born. Having observed a number of international programs that our universities have sent abroad recently, I am profoundly skeptical about the unexamined cultural biases of our educational exports.

Every society is in a different stage in the evolution of its learning system, with a varying mix of explicit and embedded goals and of indoctrination and intentional learning. As we have yet to explore the issue of how to develop a learning agenda in the United States, I can only believe that this issue is unexplored elsewhere as well.

We urgently need to move to an explicit learning system paradigm in the U.S., but other countries may have more time. If they understood the dynamism of their present learning systems, however, they could better anticipate necessary changes and prevent a crisis like ours. Given the ready availability of telecommunications and computer technology, some countries might wish to bypass some of the intermediate forms of schooling and move right on to high-tech-augmented delivery systems. The U.S. could contribute to other countries' development if we undertook exporting a learning system paradigm that was readily and more sensitively adapted to a country's condition and needs. As we adapt to the new learning paradigm more effectively in our own society, perhaps we'll have something better than pop culture to export.

CHAPTER 14

Keeping It Going

The Elusive and Humbling Art of Making Change

We live in a time of great paradoxes. No previous generation has had the understanding, consciousness, and readiness for personal, institutional, and cultural change that we have, and yet millions of us feel baffled and powerless in the face of the watershed challenges. We are blessed with a growing cadre of futurists and change agents scattered throughout our institutions, but the management of change is still an elusive and humbling art. Having dabbled at it for a quarter of a century now, I find that one out of ten efforts succeeds. This has deepened my compassion and respect for all those who risk starting a business, going out for a team, or promoting an idea and then failing. The nation needs such risk takers and should be more generous to them when they fail. My awe of St. Paul, Thomas Paine, Martin Luther King, Jr., and all the other successful change makers has grown over the years.

Watershed periods are more hospitable to change makers and change making than quiescent periods, however. Right now we are eager to reach the safe harbor of some distant future, we know that our generation must organize a once-in-a-century economic transformation, and we are preparing to do it. We are beginning to understand that we must rebuild the foundations for more effective communities and a more vital public life, and some useful prototypes are in place. We are exploring new ways to construct our personal and family lives with our new freedom and choice, ways that would have mystified our grandparents.

To meet these challenges we need the higher level of human competence which a strengthened system of human learning will produce. This book's optimistic conclusion is that the American system of

143

human learning is being transformed through millions of individuals' actions as we take on the watershed challenges in our lives, communities, companies, and institutions. My chiding message is that we can do better by accelerating the strengthening of the learning system and that we all have our work cut out for us.

The public debate centering on improving schools is confined to the old, obsolete learning paradigm. Unless we broaden it to the larger question of all the life learnings we need to meet our goals and to all the settings in which we learn, we will miss the opportunity to take an essential step toward the "good society."

It is in our nature to learn visions of the "good society" and the "good life" and then to learn the means of realizing them, but the disarray in the present learning system has made both the learning of the vision and the means to it problematical. Nevertheless, American adaptive capacities have led to a strengthened learning system based on the megatrends of sharper and more explicit goal setting in all areas of living, the expanding scope of intentional learning, the move toward greater self-directedness and responsibility, a lifelong learning commitment, and the recognition that the necessary life learnings take place in many settings. The issue now is to acknowledge these megatrends and organize to move them along more quickly.

In the introduction to Part II I described the efforts a few of us are making to accelerate the strengthening of the American learning system. As always, the translation of ideas into action begins with rather modest products. There have been a few successes and many failures. Let me now bring you up to date on what and how we are doing.

Prototypes for Change

Strengthening the Louisiana Learning System

As you will recall, the change strategy was to organize some prototype projects while disseminating the ideas around the country. The most ambitious attempt to apply the model began to take shape in Louisiana in early 1984. Gordon "Nick" Mueller, Dean of Metropolitan College at the University of New Orleans, Tony Gagliano of the Regional Planning Commission, Father Dave Boileau of the Archdiocese of New Orleans, and Brother David Sinitiere, long active on educational issues, organized to introduce Governor Edwin Edwards, just beginning his third term, to the new learning paradigm. As a consequence, Governor

Edwards is the first political leader to go beyond the narrow terms of the "education" debate and organize a process to strengthen the Louisiana learning system. The ripples of the governor's action have already begun to make their way around the country.

CLEO

Our first vehicle applying the new paradigm was CLEO, the consortium of thirty-four colleges and universities in the Philadelphia region. During the spring of 1983 the CLEO board established the promotion of the new learning paradigm as its top priority for the year ahead; this is leading to a greater evangelical effort among the member institutions to make the required adjustments. It is also leading to a stronger outreach to other community institutions to bring the paradigm to life in the region.

EMO

More particularly, CLEO is bringing the paradigm of life through the EMO concept (described in Chapter Eleven) in several different settings. The first is in the Great Valley Corporate Center and could become the model for such centers and industrial parks around the country. The second aims to supply a new set of supports to small and mid-sized businesses in the Philadelphia area. As we move through the early phases of implementing this invention, we are identifying the adjustments required in the consumer and provider institutions and are beginning to make those adjustments. We have made some new friends in the computer software community and are discussing joint ventures to produce software built on the premises of the new paradigm.

Delaware County, Pennsylvania

There have been some significant spin-offs from CLEO's presence and advocacy. Dick DeCosmo's plan to have the Delaware County Community College work with the other institutions in his county's learning system to strengthen it on a county-wide scale could lead to one of the most interesting applications in the country. When fully developed, you will find educators, business leaders, politicians, religious leaders, and civic leaders working together to sharpen goal setting and then synergizing aggregate activities to achieve those goals.

Wilmington College

One of the other CLEO alumni, Ron Watts, now vice-president of
Wilmington College, with Audrey Duberstein, his forward-looking
president, is working to reshape the structure and processes of his
college to exemplify the new learning paradigm and enable his students
to become lifelong, self-directed learners. They are moving to create
"tomorrow's college today!"

Faculty Seminar

My long dream to have Temple lead other universities in the implementation of the new paradigm ended abruptly during the spring of 1983
when the new administration decided they could do better without me.
My only regret is that the Faculty Seminar's hope to secure a major
foundation grant to apply the new paradigm was thwarted as a consequence. Having been an "itch" during most of my twenty-six years
at the institution, I would have fired me a long time ago. Change
makers need to take risks and face the consequences. Happily these
are less onerous now than they would have been twenty years ago. I
still feel affection for Temple University and wish it well. The members
of the Faculty Seminar continue to work on behalf of their vision in a
variety of ways, and time is on their side.

Other Prototypes

Another prototype is taking shape in the Scranton, Pennsylvania area
through the leadership of the Reverend Jay Springer. He is working
with some of the continuing education leadership and has involved
WVIA-TV, the local public television station. Modest beginnings, to be
sure, but beginnings nonetheless.

National Efforts

At the national level the developing coalition among community colleges, continuing educators, and corporate educators is the first step to
giving some national leadership for a strengthened learning system. By
the time this book is published, this group will have begun to alert the
nation to its new learning tasks and will have begun to expand the
coalition. While this too is a modest beginning, it demonstrates that
there is educational leadership available to meet the criticisms of the
national reports and show the way to a strengthened learning system.

A century ago, as the last shift in the learning paradigm was underway, most of the early leadership in designing the new institutions came from noneducators. We are more fortunate this time.

Community Colleges

We all should continue to keep our eyes on the nation's community colleges, for they may reach the new paradigm before the other educational sectors. Under Dale Parnell's determined leadership in their national association, and given their superior sensitivity to our rapidly changing learning needs at both national and local levels, many community colleges will become education's equivalent of the excellent companies. Local coalitions of community colleges, other continuing educators, and ASTD's corporate educators will be the base for activities and strategies to strengthen human learning in communities, counties, and regions.

Other Institutions

I suspect the education/business connection will develop rapidly but that we will also see movement in the churches and even in the media in the near future as the broader tasks of human learning become better known and understood. If the politicians help us see the tasks as a race to the future, we'll do even better.

Will We, Won't We?

But will we come to an explicit and crisp commitment to strengthen the American learning system? We can't afford to blunder through this one. Few of us will choose a lower standard of living, so the drive to transform the economy must continue. Moreover, most of us are ready for better ways to run our lives and those of our families. As we come to understand that there are better ways to structure our communities and public lives, most of us will be ready to do what it takes. I believe we'll make it happen. As in other transitional periods, there will come a joyful moment like the one Martin Luther King, Jr. described in his "I have a dream" speech—joy in having come through disarray to a new clarity of purpose and task.

As I have struggled for a sense of coherence in my own life over the years, I have been deeply moved and helped by reading Herbert Muller's three-volume series, *The History of Freedom*. Freedom is so often a code word for partisan political positions that we forget its deeper meaning in the evolution of our species. Muller's first volume gave me a vivid sense of how the ancient Minoan farmer was imprisoned in his own ignorance, fearful of all the dangerous spirits threatening his crops and his own existence. The drama of the subsequent evolution of human freedom over the millenia has continued to stir my imagination more than any other aspect of our precarious existence.

Each of us must engage our inherited freedom to keep it in trust for the generations to come. This is both a personal and communal obligation, as the history of this century amply demonstrates. Freedom is a renewable resource as long as we nurture it. New dimensions of freedom are now coming into sight, and it is up to our generation to engage them by strengthening the American learning system. That is the basic message I have to offer.

Having acknowledged my debt to Muller and all the others who have shaped my thought, I conclude with the maxim Justice Holmes delivered in an 1884 Memorial Day address which has sustained me throughout my life:

"As life is action and passion it is required of a man that he should share the action and passion of his time, at peril of being judged not to have lived."

Annotated Bibliography

A

Allen, Frederick Lewis. *Only Yesterday*. New York: Harper & Row, 1964.

————. *Since Yesterday*. New York: Harper Bros., 1940.

————. *The Big Change*. New York: Harper, 1952. Popular social histories of the twenties, thirties, and the first half of the twentieth century. Useful and entertaining reminders of the scope of change in American life during this century.

Argyris, Chris, and Schon, Donald A. *Theory in Practice*. San Francisco: Jossey-Bass, 1974. An exploration of the "theories of action" that are involved in human interaction. This study gives us a dynamic and holistic way to describe and analyze human behavior.

Ariès, Phillipe. *Centuries of Childhood*. Translated by Robert Baldick. New York: Alfred A. Knopf, 1962. A landmark study of the changing definition of childhood throughout human history. It provides a foundation of understanding from which we can decide how to define childhood in our own time.

Auletta, Ken. *The Underclass*. New York: Random House, 1982. A vivid and depressing description of the contemporary American underclass. Current approaches are clearly inadequate. Provides support for a systemic approach to human learning and development.

B

Berger, Brigette, and Berger, Peter L. *The War Over the Family*. New York: Doubleday, 1983. After the decades of self-fulfilling individualism, the Bergers' argue the centrality of the family in contemporary society and make a variety of proposals to strengthen the nuclear family.

Berger, Peter, and Neuhaus, Richard J. *To Empower People*. Washington, D.C.: American Enterprise Institute for Public Policy Research, 1977. A useful and powerful reminder that the "mediating structures" of family, community, church, voluntary associations, and subcultures are vital in meeting human needs and ought to be strengthened through public policy. Provided the Reagan administration with a policy base, though not one that was successfully engaged.

Bolles, Richard N. *What Color Is Your Parachute?* Berkeley, Calif.: Ten Speed Press, 1978.

———. *The Three Boxes of Life.* Berkeley, Calif.: Ten Speed Press, 1978. These delightful and effective guides to career and life planning have done more to help people take charge of their lives than any other publications. Someday the mainstream institutions will begin to pay attention!

Botkin, James, Elmandjra, Mahdi, and Malitza, Mircea. *No Limits to Learning: Bridging the Human Gap.* London: Pergamon Press, 1979. Another startling study sponsored by the Club of Rome in which the learning process in societies throughout the world is characterized as inadequate to get the planet to a safe future. Useful proposals to stimulate anticipatory and innovative learning are made.

Bronfonbrenner, Urie. *Two Worlds of Childhood.* New York: Russell Sage Foundation, 1970.

———. *The Ecology of Human Development.* Cambridge, Mass.: Harvard University Press, 1979. One of America's most gifted child development specialists compares American and Russian child rearing and then offers a theoretical framework for human development viewed in ecological terms.

Burns, James MacGregor. *Leadership.* New York: Harper & Row, 1978. It is in this volume that Professor Burns sensitizes us to the distinction between "transactional" and "transforming" leadership. Wouldn't it be helpful to have a little more transforming leadership to guide us through the new American watershed?

C

Carnegie Council on Policy Studies in Higher Education. *Three Thousand Futures.* San Francisco: Jossey-Bass, 1980. This summary volume of the Council discusses in fairly bleak terms the challenges facing American higher education in the next two decades. Although it seeks to rally the troops to face the challenges in a creative and aggressive manner, it falls short because of its failure to question the legitimacy of the present learning paradigm.

Chickering, Arthur W. *The Modern American College.* San Francisco: Jossey-Bass, 1981. This landmark book explores the expanding scope of intentional learning and its implications for reform of the college curriculum. Had higher education paid attention to Chickering's argument, it might be on the road to greater vitality.

Churchman, C. West. *The Systems Approach.* New York: Dell, 1968. A primer on understanding and managing people, problems, functions, and institutions as "systems." As you read it you'll be impressed by the degree to which the systems approach has pervaded our thinking in recent decades.

Cremin, Lawrence A. *Traditions of American Education.* New York: Basic Books, 1977. The nation's premier educational historian summarizes his work in this small volume of lectures. He continues to remind us that there are many learning settings, not just the school. The new American watershed may finally lead us to pay attention.

Crunden, Robert M. *Ministers of Reform: The Progressives' Achievement in American Civilization, 1889–1920.* New York: Basic Books, 1983. This most timely book reviews the rise of the Progressive movement in response to the challenges of the last American watershed period a century ago. It reminds us that "movements" are the product of caring, thinking, and active people.

D

Deal, Terrence E., and Kennedy, Allan A. *Corporate Culture.* Reading, Mass.: Addison-Wesley, 1982. The kickoff volume on corporate cultures from the McKinsey think-tank that has been so catalytic in the management revolution now taking place.

Donzelot, Jacques. *The Policing of Families.* New York: Pantheon Books, 1979. Another in the continuing stream of incisive French social histories. Donzelot describes the ways in which the state and the professions, often mindlessly, shape the concept and functioning of families. A humbling reminder that good intentions do not guarantee good results.

E

Etzioni, Amitai. *An Immodest Agenda.* New York: McGraw-Hill, 1983. While acknowledging the urgency of rebuilding America's economy, Etzioni argues that the rebuilding of community is equally important. As always, his analysis is incisive and his recommendations right on target. One of 1983's most important books.

F

Fromm, Erich. *Escape from Freedom.* New York: Holt, Rinehart and Winston, 1976.

———. *Man for Himself.* New York: Holt, Rinehart and Winston, 1947. One of my heroes during my student days, Fromm helped us understand the corrosive effects of unengaged freedom and the need to develop a new set of human competencies in our age of expanding choices. Fromm's thought is even more relevant in the eighties than it was in the forties.

H

Harrington, Michael. *The Other America.* New York: Macmillan, 1960. An example of the right book at the right time. By painting a vivid picture of the scope of poverty at a moment when Americans were ready to be generous, Harrington helped build the foundation for all of the social programs of the sixties. Auletta's *The Underclass* did not elicit a similar sentiment in the eighties.

Hawken, Paul. *The Next Economy.* New York: Holt, Rinehart and Winston, 1983. As the nation fumbles for an economic strategy, Hawken proposes a comprehensive approach based on the reduction of mass and energy and the greater application of information to product and service development. By "smartening up" the economy we just might build on our human resources and improve our competitiveness.

J

Jacobs, Jane. *The Death and Life of Great American Cities*. New York: Random House, 1961. An upbeat book that appeared during the dark days of the urban crisis in the sixties and offered a strategy and a number of practical suggestions for improving life in the big city.

Jones, Landon Y. *Great Expectations: America and the Baby-Boom Generation*. New York: Coward, McCann & Geoghegan, 1980. This is the story of America's baby-boom generation and its passage through the lifespan. Jones describes the shift as the baby-boomers approach the middle years from high expectations to the sobering realities and uncertainties of today. I believe this is one of the important books of the decade.

K

Knox, Alan. *Adult Development and Learning*. San Francisco: Jossey-Bass, 1977. This book by one of the leaders of American continuing education made a special contribution in expanding the scope of intentional learning to include role, value, and affective aspects. It is also a veritable compendium of material that can be applied by continuing education practitioners.

Kuhn, Thomas S. *The Structure of Scientific Revolutions*. Chicago: University of Chicago Press, 1970. One of the landmark books in its description of the process whereby the paradigms of science change. Never a neat and precise intellectual process, but accompanied by political and psychological struggle, the metaphor of the paradigm shift has moved beyond science to portray the movement of basic ideas in applied areas as well. Thank you, Dr. Kuhn.

L

Lasch, Christopher. *The Culture of Narcissism*. New York: W. W. Norton Co., 1978.

———. *Haven in a Heartless World*. New York: Basic Books, 1977. These two critical studies in social history explore the recent growth of a hedonistic individualism in American society and the debilitating role of the helping professions and social policy on the family. Lasch is one of the most trenchant commentators on the American scene.

M

Mankiewicz, Frank. *Remote Control*. New York: Times Books, 1978. An interesting book of analysis and commentary on the role of television in American life. Concerned about the growth and influence of the medium in recent decades, Mankiewicz offers the critical image of television as an overly powerful "troubadour." I thank Mr. Mankiewicz for the image.

Mead, Margaret. *Culture and Commitment*. Garden City, N.Y.: Doubleday & Co., 1978. Dr. Mead's last book offers her original analysis of the fundamental shifts taking place in American culture. She vividly portrays the cleavage between pre- and post-World War II generations in the shift from traditional authority to the authority of the contemporary generation.

Muller, Herbert. *Freedom in the Ancient World*. New York: Harper & Row, 1961.

————. *Freedom in the Western World*. New York: Harper & Row, 1963.

————. *Freedom in the Modern World*. New York: Harper & Row, 1966. This English professor has written a series of entrancing history books with a central focus on the emergence and evolution of freedom. In my struggle to understand our own time, Muller has been one of the important mentors for me.

Murphy, Gardner. *Human Potentialities*. New York: Basic Books, 1958. Murphy's sense that we have only begun to develop the manifold potentialities of our species conveys a marvelous optimism for us to build on. As coming from one of the century's great psychologists Murphy's conclusion is hardly Pollyannaish; he recognized that we could easily go the other way.

N

Naisbett, John. *Megatrends*. New York: Warner Books, 1982. Based on the culling of media materials, Naisbett and his associates offer ten key trends that are taking us to the future. While nothing is ever certain about futuristic projections, the book's optimism and its capacity to motivate us to create the future make it a major contribution to the evolutionary process.

Nisbet, Robert. *History of the Idea of Progress*. New York: Basic Books, 1980. A marvelous exploration of the evolution of the idea of progress from the Greeks to the present. Mostly history, but also social commentary, Nisbet's study concludes in deep pessimism about the future. A useful counterpoint to the perennial optimists.

O

O'Toole, James. *Making America Work*. New York: Continuum, 1981. The author's analysis of the productivity problem in the American economy takes him past a narrow economic fix such as the attempts to transplant Japanese management techniques imply. He sees both the problem and the solution in American culture. Right on target.

P

Packard, Vance. *Our Endangered Children*. Boston: Little, Brown and Company, 1983. Another volume from the most productive social critic of the postwar decades. With a wide lens he surveys the conditions confronting children in the growing-up process today. He narrows his lens and provides a valuable analysis of such issues as working mothers, day care, etc.

Peters, Thomas J., and Waterman, Robert H., Jr. *In Search of Excellence*. New York: Harper & Row, 1982. This runaway best seller not only provides us with "lessons from America's best-run companies," but, even more importantly, it is the right book at the right time helping to catalyze the economic transformation.

R

Reich, Charles. *The Greening of America*. New York: Random House, 1970. A book that built on the sugarplum visions of the counter-culture and suggested that we were entering a new stage of humanness now that all of the economic problems had been solved. Seemed a lot more possible then than now.

Revel, Jean. *Without Marx or Jesus*. (Translated by J. F. Bernard.) Garden City, N.Y.: Doubleday & Co., 1971. A good example of the right book at the wrong time. A French bouquet to the capacity of American society to adapt and evolve, it was published at a time when we were particularly self-critical and couldn't respond to foreign compliments. Worth rereading.

S

Salisbury, Harrison. *Without Fear or Favor*. New York: New York Times, 1980. A detailed history of the *New York Times* complete with a description of undercover relationships between the paper and government. Salisbury crowns the history with what I think is a very necessary moral inquiry into the proper role of the media in a free society.

Schumaker, E. F. *Small Is Beautiful*. New York: Harper & Row, 1973. In an age when big government, large multi-national corporations, and an interrelated, international economy are the overwhelming metaphors feeding powerlessness at the personal level, Schumaker reminds us that smallness may be a virtue, even an economic virtue, and that the retreat into powerlessness is not inevitable.

Sennett, Richard. *Authority*. New York: Alfred A. Knopf, 1980. An excellent study of the shifting character of authority in a modern society. Deals with the contemporary issue of how, having diminished much of our traditional authority, we wish to organize our authority structures to meet our goals.

Sheehy, Gail. *Passages*. New York: E. P. Dutton, 1974. Building on the work of Daniel Levinson and others, Sheehy expanded the consciousness of the American people to the reality of our development through the lifespan and to the need to guide and manage that development. A fundamental contribution to the intentional learning trend.

T

Toffler, Alvin. *Future Shock*. New York: Random House, 1970.

———. *The Third Wave*. New York: William Morrow and Co., 1980.

———. *Previews and Premises*. New York: William Morrow and Co., 1983. America's most prolific futurist has done more to turn our attention to the future than any other author. In these books he has sensitized us to the likely dimensions of that future, while also reminding us that each of us can have a hand in the final design of that future.

de Toqueville, Alexis. *Democracy in America*. New York: Washington Square, 1964. This Frenchman's description of life in America during the 1830s is one of those classics that deserves to be reread from time to time. Its depiction of the feisty spirit of the early Americans provides a continuing challenge to every generation to remain faithful to that spirit.

Tuchman, Barbara. *A Distant Mirror*. New York: Alfred A. Knopf, 1978. More than a marvelous account of life and change during the fourteenth century, this is Ms. Tuchman's reminder to our generation that the species has lived through periods of great change in the past and that we might do a little better this time.

V

Veysey, Lawrence. *The Emergence of the American University*. Chicago: University of Chicago Press, 1965. The basic study on the fundamental redesign of American higher education a century ago as a response to the challenges of the last American watershed. The fact that the Academy never came to synthesis and yet had a most successful century is a delightful irony. Also a reminder that some of our icons are transient bric-a-brac. Required reading and rereading for anyone who cares about higher education.

W

Weiner, Norbert. *The Human Use of Human Beings*. New York: Houghton Mifflin, 1950. This popular adaptation of the landmark *Cybernetics* was Weiner's attempt to bring the notion of self-correcting systems and its application to the public. One of those benchmark books that needs to be reread from time to time to see how far we have come—and how far we have yet to go.

Will, George. *Statecraft as Soulcraft*. New York: Simon and Schuster, 1983. Another right book at the right time. Will properly argues that the premises of the American government, which arose out of the embedded premises of eighteenth-century American culture, may not be right for our time. His argument that the development of human character is a public concern provides a rationale for an updated political agenda. It also is supportive of my thesis that the human learning system needs to become an object of policy and guidance.

Wilson, Sloan. *The Man in the Gray Flannel Suit*. New York: Simon and Schuster, 1955. The fifties novel that put the spotlight on the emptiness of corporate success in that era. What a difference a generation makes!

Winn, Marie. *Children Without Childhood*. New York: Pantheon Books, 1983. Winn holds up the mirror to a series of inadvertent shifts in the way Americans are raising their children. The loss of the period of protection which has characterized proper child rearing over the past few centuries holds some dire consequences but is within our capacity to change—if we wish to.

Y

Yankelovich, Daniel. *New Rules*. New York: Random House, 1981. If I had to choose the most important book of the decade, it would be this one. Yankelovich's portrayal of the "shifting plates of American culture" and his perceptive analysis of the shifts for the economy, personal, and family lives provides the best foundation from which personal and collective understanding and action can be developed and taken.

Index